ERIN D

A Beautiful Story

MAKING GOD'S STORY YOURS

LifeWay Press
Nashville, Tennessee

ISBN: 978-1-4300-6920-1
Item Number: 005793034

Dewey Decimal Classification Number: 248.83
Subject Heading: RELIGION / Christian Ministry / Youth

Printed in the United States of America

Student Ministry Publishing
LifeWay Resources
One LifeWay Plaza
Nashville, TN 37234-0144

We believe that the Bible has God for its author; salvation for its end; and truth, without any mixture of error, for its matter and that all Scripture is totally true and trustworthy. To review LifeWay's doctrinal guideline, please visit www.lifeway.com/doctrinalguideline.

TABLE OF CONTENTS

ABOUT THE AUTHOR

ERIN DAVIS is a popular author, blogger, and speaker who loves to see women of all ages run to the deep well of God's Word. She is the author of many books and Bible studies including *Connected*, *True Princess*, *Beautiful Encounters*, and the *My Name Is Erin* series. When she's not writing, you can find Erin chasing chickens and children on her small farm in the Midwest.

HOW TO USE THIS STUDY

This book contains eight weekly group studies. Each session consists of a group guide followed by four days of personal study. There is also a leader guide in the back of this study with helpful tips to use during group time. As you close each session, encourage students to complete the homework days that follow. Once students have completed this study, they will have discovered New Testament truths through the lives of ten Old Testament women.

HOW TO ANNOTATE

Throughout this study, I'll reference journaling and annotating. These are the methods I use most often during my personal Bible study. It's okay to write in your Bible. You can write out questions, prayers, lists, and even create drawings that relate to the text. Choose a writing tool that won't bleed through the pages such as colored pencils or felt tip markers. The goal isn't to preserve your Bible for use in a museum display some day. The goal is to get into God's Word and get God's Word into you.

INTRODUCTION

Your life is the pen God is using to write *A Beautiful Story*.

Before you wrap yourself up in the warm fuzzy feelings of this sentiment, let me clarify. The main character of your story, and of mine, might surprise you. Who we are and how we live is the lower story. This study is an invitation to lift your eyes. Look up. See the higher arc of your story and the stories of those who have gone before you. When we widen the lens, we see how each of us joins a long line of rotating characters whose lives point to bigger, more significant truths. Ultimately, our stories are not about us, but about the author of every narrative—our stories are about God.

In this study, you'll dig deep into the lives of ten women. Some of them you've likely heard of (like Eve), and a few of them might be new to you (like Gomer), but set aside first impressions. They rarely reveal the whole story. I invite you to look closer. Assume the role of a journalist. Take a second look. Find the clues that point past how each woman lived and toward who God is.

Together, we'll peel back the layers of each woman's story to find how it is:

- less about what she accomplished on her own and more about what God accomplished through her.
- less about who liked her and more about who loved her with an everlasting, steadfast love.
- less about perfection and more about redemption.
- less about grabbing the spotlight for herself and more about using her life to show God's glory.

These women's lives span thousands of years on the timeline of humanity, yet they are stitched together with the same thread that weaves in and out of ours. God is the author of every pen stroke. He's the hero of every tale. As we sift through each story, I hope you'll often circle back to your own. How has God marked your story? How can you use your own life to point to something greater?

With those questions in mind, lets dig in. Our story begins like all the good ones do: Once upon a time.

God Speaks: A Beautiful Beginning

So God created man in his own image;
he created him in the image of God;
he created them male and female.
GENESIS 1:27

STRETCH

Maybe you didn't realize when you picked up this study that you were also enrolling in Journalism 101. Don't panic! This is a crash course and there will be no papers due, no tests to take, and no lectures to listen to. To ace this class you'll only need to learn one lesson: It's the journalism principle of the inverted pyramid.

I first learned about the inverted pyramid in journalism school. It works like this: When telling a story, share the most important information first. Usually, this involves the who, what, when, where, and why. Then, begin sharing information that's less important, things like commentary from witnesses, quotes, or minor details. Finally, the bottom of the pyramid (it's upside down, remember?) is reserved for the parts of the story that are non-essential. These are the details only really interested readers care about.

You'll get to practice answering questions about the lives of ten women throughout this study. As you read about them in God's Word, train yourself to look for the who, what, when, where, and why. You'll record your answers in the Story I.D. chart for each session. If charting God's Word is new to you, this may feel awkward at first—it will certainly take a bit more effort than simply reading through a passage once or twice. I want it to change how you think and respond to God.

As you investigate, remember that the people in the Bible aren't there to show us what perfect Christians look like. Their stories do show us that God loves and uses people of all kinds in every moment of history.

Train yourself to ask these questions:

- **Who:** Who is this about? (name, family, etc.)
- **What:** What defines her? (personality, characteristics, likes, dislikes, etc.)
- **When:** What is the historical and cultural context? What happened before and after this?
- **Where:** Where did she live?
- **Why:** Why is this important? Remember to invert the pyramid here. The most important detail of each story is what it reveals about God, not what it reveals about the woman we're investigating.

Alright, journalists! Let's begin with an easy one. Her story starts at the very beginning.

STORY I.D.

Using the chart below, fill in what you already know about Eve. Then, check out Genesis 1–4. Use the information in the passage to fill in any details you missed.

Who   Eve

What

When

Where

Why

DIGGING DEEPER

Who am I? This question seems to haunt every girl. We run anywhere and everywhere looking for answers, but this constant running often sends us spiraling down the wrong path.

Take a few minutes to list who each of these influences think you should be.

The Culture. Based on the messages you see in magazines, television shows, and through social media, who does the culture say you should be?

Your family. How do your parents and siblings define you?

Yourself. Who do you think you should be?

These are just three of the countless voices with an opinion about who you are. But those voices often contradict each other. The culture wants you to be/think/act/dream one way, and your parents have a totally different idea. You may define your identity one way, and your friends may want you to be someone else completely. Before long, you start to feel like the rope in a giant game of tug of war. When we look to the wrong sources to tell us who we are, we may even feel stretched to the point of breaking.

We need a new game plan. We must train ourselves to look to the right source.

WHO GETS TO DECIDE?

Fast forward a few years, and imagine you are the creator of an invention that will change the world. Maybe it's a groundbreaking piece of technology that allows us to travel at light speed. Maybe you've developed a machine that can cure cancer with the push of a button. Maybe you've finally invented a way to keep from losing only one shoe. It doesn't really matter what the imaginary invention is, what matters is that *you* created it.

Now, imagine you've planned a big event to unveil your invention to the world. All of the major news networks are live streaming the launch. This is your moment!

- Who would you pick to explain your invention?
- Would you let the news crews who have never seen your product in action explain what it is?
- Would you ask some friends who like you but haven't spent months partnering with you in developing this product?
- How about the invention itself? Would you uncover it in front of your audience and hope it could speak for itself?

Of course not!

As the creator, you are the best person to define the invention. You are the expert on what it is and what it can do. Eve's story helps us see how the same principle applies to our own identities.

The creation story reminds us that God is the Creator of everything around us. God spoke *everything* into existence. Every fish in the sea, every bird in the air, and every zebra that wanders the African plains was designed and created by God.

John 1:3 says it this way:

> *All things were created through him, and apart from him not one thing was created that has been created.*

Who is the "him" in this passage?

If you guessed Jesus, you're spot on! You may think of Jesus as the God of the New Testament, but when we dig deeper into the Old Testament, we see Him *everywhere*. As we study God's Word, we discover that the Old Testament is like a gigantic neon arrow that points *forward* toward Christ's coming, and the New Testament is like a gigantic neon arrow that points *backward* toward His life, death, and resurrection. He is smack dab in the middle of the most important story ever written. This is a critical piece of the puzzle as you look for the higher story in the lives of the women we'll consider through this study.

Let me show you what I mean. As we take a deeper look, try thinking through the story like a journalist.

Write out Genesis 1:26.

God doesn't have to plot, plan, and beta test His creations. But let's think back to our invention example and imagine this passage is like the brainstorming phase of creation.

> Keeping in mind that Adam had not been created yet, who was God talking to in this passage?

God was talking to Himself. God the Father, God the Son, and God the Holy Spirit were all present at creation. As we comb back through Genesis 1 looking for clues, we see the Father creating and the Spirit hovering (v. 2). John 1:3 helps us see that Jesus was also present and that everything was made through Him.

Keep this in mind as we pivot from the creation of the world to the creation of Eve.

> Write out Genesis 1:27.

> This passage seems to repeat the same thought three times. What is the main idea?

In this verse, God used a teaching strategy with us. He repeated an important idea because He wants you to pay attention. It's as if He is saying, "Don't miss this! It's too important!" Theologians call this passage the *Imago Dei*. It simply means all men and women bear God's image. We'll take a closer look at the *Imago Dei* in your devotions this week, but for now lets zero in on two key ideas:

1. God created Eve.
2. God created Eve in His own image.

Since God created Eve in His own image, He defined her identity, just like an inventor gets to define the invention. We may have some ideas about who Eve was or who she should have been, but ultimately God is the one who assigned Eve's identity, and God is the one who assigns your identity.

> Look back through Eve's story. Who did God say she was in each of the following verses?

Genesis 1:27

Genesis 1:31

Genesis 2:18

Go back to your Story I.D. for Eve. Fill in any new information you've uncovered.

TALK ABOUT IT

Discuss the following questions with your group.

How does the Imago Dei impact the way you view your own identity? How does it impact the way you see others?

Did you see anything in Eve's story you had not noticed before?

What did you learn about God's character through Eve's story?

THINK ABOUT IT

As we will discover in this week's devotions, when Eve allowed someone other than God to define her identity, she found herself in deep trouble. Her story sends up a warning flare for each of us. Like Eve, you were made in the image of God. You are a living, breathing portrait of the *Imago Dei*. From the beginning, God's plan was for you to tell the world about *Him*.

Since you were made by God and have been marked with the image of God, choose to turn up the volume on God's voice and turn down the volume of the other voices around you when it comes to defining who you are.

Take some time now to journal a prayer to God. Confess your tendency to define your identity based on your own perceptions or the influence of others. Since He is your Creator, ask Him to help you see yourself as He sees you.

Who? The Imago Dei

In addition to charting eight Old Testament women throughout this study, you will occasionally be asked to chart additional people including other characters from the Bible story we're investigating or individuals from church history. In this session, I'd like you to chart someone you know especially well: yourself.

Who _____

What _____

When _____

Where _____

Why

When most people think of Eve, they tend to define her with a list of firsts.

- She was the first woman to ever live.
- She was the first wife and mother.
- She was the first person to sin.

It's easy to boil down Eve's entire identity to that last bullet point. It's true that Adam and Eve sinned and in doing so, they sent a shock wave through history that we are still dealing with today. We'll look more closely at the impact of sin in tomorrow's devotion. For now, let's circle back to the *Imago Dei*. If you need a refresher, check out Genesis 1:27.

Imago Dei translates to "image of God." God created everything: planets, stars, oceans, continents, animals, plants, and so on. But the *Imago Dei* is unique to us as humans. In all of creation, we are the only ones made in the image of God.

While that should make us feel special (because we are), remember to look for the higher story. The point of the *Imago Dei* isn't to bolster our self-esteem. It's not about our outer beauty. The lower story is who we are. The higher story is who God is. We understand our identity by understanding who He is. We have value because we bear the image of the God of the universe.

Circle back to the chart you made about yourself. Reframe your identity with the *Imago Dei* at the forefront of your mind. Rework the chart with these questions in mind.

- Who does God say you are?
- What story does He want your life to tell?
- When did God give value to you?
- Where does your story fit in the higher story of who God is?
- Why did God create you?

Who

What

When

Where

Why

As we examine the women of the Old Testament, we will zero in on the *Imago Dei* over and over. Learning to see ourselves and the people around us as image bearers is a game changer. Eve isn't defined by her relationships or her mistakes; she is defined by her Creator. In the same way, you are not defined by *your* relationships, *your* mistakes, *your* gifts, *your* talents, *your* dreams, *your* beauty, *your* flaws. You are defined by your Creator.

A reporter's job is to uncover the truth. In this session, I challenge you to uncover the truth about your identity by digging deep into God's Word.

Look up the following passages. Use the truth found in each verse to complete the "I am" statement.

Matthew 5:13-15 says I am...

John 15:15-16 says I am...

Galatians 3:26 says I am...

Ephesians 2:10 says I am...

1 Thessalonians 1:4 says I am...

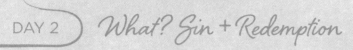

What? Sin + Redemption

Read Genesis 2:8-25.

> What words would you use to describe Adam and Eve's reality in these verses?

If you chose words like perfect, beautiful, or peaceful, you've got the right picture.

Adam and Eve were created by God with tender care. There was no suffering or strain to be found in a single corner of Eden. Everything about their existence was "very good" (Gen. 1:31).

> Take a moment to scroll through today's top headlines. Do you see any remnants of Eden? Or does it feel more like paradise has been lost?

> Think about your own life. Does it seem filled with purpose, blessings, and a God-given mission? Or are your days jammed with pressure, stress, and mundane tasks?

The same God who created Eve in His own image, created you in His image. The God who spoke our planet into perfect existence is the same God who rules and reigns over our broken world. God hasn't changed, but it seems everything else has. Eve's story is critical to helping us understand why.

In the beginning, Eve's life was perfect. If we fast-forward, we see that it didn't stay that way for long. In just a few chapters, Adam and Eve's stories took a dramatic and devastating turn. They were evicted from their home in paradise and forced to live a harsh life outside the gates of Eden. Their oldest son, Cain, murdered their younger son, Abel. Life went from "very good" to very bad for Adam and Eve with a single bite of forbidden fruit.

You likely already know the story, but let's revisit it while digging deep. Read Genesis 3. Be on the lookout for clues to the higher story. Here are some questions to get you thinking:

- Where was God when Eve was tempted?
- What was the serpent trying to convince Eve about God?
- How might Eve have responded differently to the serpent if she remembered she was made in God's image?
- How did God respond to Eve's sin?

  What words would you use to describe Adam and Eve's reality after the fall?

It's tough to describe how devastating sin is. Since we've never known the sin-free life Adam and Eve temporarily enjoyed in Eden, our hearts and minds can barely comprehend the peace, joy, and unity they experienced before the fall. We see the world through sin-tainted glasses.

  Read the curse handed down by God in Genesis 3:14-19. Rewrite this passage in your own words, noting how you've felt the impact of sin in your own life.

As we read Eve's story, it is tempting to see her sin as the end of all that is good. But that's not the whole story. Like us, Eve's story is marked by two key themes: sin and redemption. We'll explore the meaning of redemption throughout the pages of this study. Eve's identity is not defined by who she was but by whose image she bears. The theme of her story is not the fall but God's merciful redemption.

Jesus is a direct descendant of Adam. It's true that Adam and Eve's sin has impacted every generation since the Garden, but it's also true that a Redeemer has been born in their family line to rescue us from the impact of sin.

Jesus was present at Eve's creation. He marked her with His image. Thousands of years later, He paid the price for Eve's sin (and ours) through His death on the cross, making a way for us to be set free from the curse of sin.

Right after God passed down the curse, Eve got a new name. It seems like a strange response to all that just happened, but it's a beautiful reminder to look for the higher story. If we zero in on Eve's sin, we get stuck in the lower story. Look up. See how her life points to God's goodness and grace.

What name did Adam give his wife in Genesis 3:20?

Eve's name means "life-giver." Adam gave her this name because "she was the mother of all the living." Yes, Eve sinned. Sin always leads to death. But even in the shadow of sin and death, Eve's story is about life. Her name tells the story of the Life-giver. Does yours?

When?
The Beginning and the End

Great stories have great beginnings. See if you can match these famous first lines with the right story.

"It's a truth universally acknowledged, that a single man in possession of a good fortune must be in want of a wife."

Charlotte's Web by E.B. White

"It was the best of times, it was the worst of times."

The Voyage of the Dawn Treader by C.S. Lewis

"There was a boy called Eustace Clarence Scrubb, and he almost deserved it."

A Tale of Two Cities by Charles Dickens

"Where's Papa going with that ax?"

Pride and Prejudice by Jane Austen

Write out Genesis 1:1.

This is the beginning of Eve's story. It is the beginning of yours too. It's such a simple truth, but one we are prone to forget. The first verse of the first book of the Bible doesn't start with "In the beginning, Eve ..." or "In the beginning, Adam ..." Eve's story begins with God. Your story begins with God. This truth is more important than you may realize. Let's dig a little deeper.

Fill in the blanks to summarize the following verses.

Jesus is the _____ of the church, the _____, and the _____ "from the dead." He has "_____ _____ in everything." **COLOSSIANS 1:18**

"I am the _____ and the _____," says the Lord God, "the one who _____ , who _____ , and who is _____ _____, the Almighty." **REVELATION 1:8**

> "I am the _____ and the _____,
> the first and the last, the _____ and the
> _____." REVELATION 22:13

God describes Himself as the *Alpha* and *Omega*, the *beginning* and the *end*. Every story begins and ends with Him. If Eve's life began with her birth and ended forever with her death, it would be a sad and simple story. The same is true for you. If the life you live between your first cry and your last was the only story you ever got to tell, it would feel more like a footnote than a great novel. This truth can lead to two reactions in our hearts.

1. It can make us feel insignificant, like our stories don't matter.

2. It can make us feel significant because we are a part of something huge.

I hope you will choose to see God's truth through the lens of the second option. When we see ourselves as a part of the bigger story—the story of God and His work among His people—our story starts to take on real significance. He invites us to be a part of something so much bigger than what we can accomplish in the days He gives us on Earth. We are a part of a story that goes on into eternity.

> God's story is as complex and beautiful as He is, but it is possible to boil it down to the big idea. Look up the first verse of the Bible (Gen. 1:1) and the last two verses of the Bible (Rev. 22:20-21). Record them as a single paragraph.

Consider this the Twitter version of God's truth. The story of humanity began when God created us, and it ends when He returns for us. All of us are somewhere between that great beginning and the best ending ever written. God holds and controls the beginning of your days and the end. What a comforting truth!

Psalm 139:5 is a favorite passage of Scripture for me. It promises that God has "encircled me" and "placed [His] hand on me." He is all around me. There is no me without Him.

As you close today's lesson, spend some time praying through Psalm 139. Thank God for His promises. Worship Him for who He is: the Alpha and Omega, the beginning and the end. Ask Him to help you live out the bigger story of who He is instead of focusing on the smaller story of who you are.

The Bigger Story

Gospel is a word you will read often on the pages of this study. If you grew up in the church, it's likely a word you've heard many times before. But what is the gospel, exactly? That's something we need to clear up before we go much further.

I'll let you go first. Use the space below to define the gospel. (No Googling or asking for help.) It's okay to struggle with this. The gospel is an idea of cosmic significance. It's not easy to sum it up in a few sentences. Let's try anyway.

The Gospel is:

Before we dig too much deeper, let's anchor ourselves with another important truth. Summarize Galatians 1:6-9.

It seems that misunderstanding the basics of the gospel is not a new problem. Paul wrote these words to the church in Galatia. These were Christians who seemed to be struggling to understand the gospel. Paul's prayer for these believers was that they would have a clear understanding of the gospel. I am praying the same thing for you.

What clues do we find about the definition of the gospel from this passage?

According to verse 7, how many versions of the gospel exist?

Paul corrected the Galatians because they were wrongly believing other gospels, then he stopped in his tracks and wrote, "not that there is another gospel" (v. 7). There is only one gospel. If we keep reading this verse we discover it is "the gospel of Christ."

Pastor Tim Keller defines the gospel this way:

> The "gospel" is the good news that through Christ the power of God's kingdom has entered history to renew the whole world. When we believe and rely on Jesus' work and record (rather than ours) for our relationship to God, that kingdom power comes upon us and begins to work through us.[1]

And pastor John Piper sums the gospel up in a single sentence.

> The Gospel is the news that Jesus Christ, the Righteous One, died for our sins and rose again, eternally triumphant over all his enemies, so that there is now no condemnation for those who believe, but only everlasting joy.[2]

What do these two definitions have in common? How do they line up with Paul's words in Galatians 2?

Just like Jesus is the theme of every story, He is the hero of the gospel. While the gospel is certainly huge in its significance, its definition is surprisingly simple.

1. We are sinners.

2. Christ is our Savior.

3. Only through Him are we released from the punishment of sin and free to spend eternity with our Creator.

Where does the story of the gospel begin? Let's retrace our steps to Eve and the garden for the answer.

Jesus is essential to the gospel, but the gospel didn't start when Jesus came to earth as a baby. Remember from the Digging Deeper section of this week that Jesus was present at the beginning of creation. He has always been included in this story. The truth of the gospel arrived on the scene shortly after He spoke the world into existence.

Review Genesis 3:1-7.

The first *tenet*, or *principle*, of the gospel is that we are sinners. Here we see that truth on full display. Eve sinned by taking the forbidden fruit and disobeying God's law. As daughters of Eve, we repeat her mistakes through the generations. But the gospel gives us hope.

What did God do for Eve in Genesis 3:21?

He clothed her. This is actually a beautiful picture of the gospel.

Read Isaiah 61:10. What does God clothe His people in?

As His children we wear "garments of salvation" and "the robe of righteousness." Eve's story is our story. She sinned and God clothed and cared for her. We sin and He still gives us clean garments that we don't deserve and welcomes us into His kingdom.

End this week's lesson by writing out a prayer to God, thanking Him for transforming your story into a gospel story.

God Sees: A Beautiful Knowing

*So she named the Lord who
spoke to her: "You are El-roi."*
GENESIS 16:13a

STRETCH

Maybe you've heard the story of the blind men and the elephant. If you haven't, it goes something like this:

> A group of blind men encounter an elephant. I don't know why they were blind or how they found themselves so close to an elephant, but it's a parable (a story with a moral) so bear with me. One man touches the elephant's tusk and decides the animal is cold and hard. Another man touches the elephant's trunk and decides the animal is long and snakelike. A final man touches the elephant's ears and decides it's hairy and flat. They were all touching the same elephant the only difference was their point of view.

Point of view (let's call it POV for short) matters when we're digging into God's Word too. Let me show you what I mean with a story that centers around an epic cat fight. (Nope, girls don't just fight in middle school. They fought in the Bible too.)

Grab your Bible and read Genesis 16. Read the entire chapter a couple of times, paying close attention to the POV.

First, read the chapter focusing on the POV of Sarai, Abraham's wife.

What challenges did Sarai face?

Now, read the chapter again focusing on the POV of Hagar, Sarai's servant.

What challenges did Hagar face?

The facts of this story remain the same, but perceptions change based on the POV of each character. Looking at Scripture this way trains our eyes to see details we might have otherwise missed. It's a great strategy to practice as you learn to approach God's Word as a journalist would.

STORY I.D.

Using the following chart, fill in what you've learned about Hagar. Refer back to Genesis 16 as often as you need to.

Who   Hagar

What

When

Where

Why

DIGGING DEEPER

Favorite flower? *Daisy.*

Favorite color? *Yellow.*

Favorite car? *T-top corvette.*

This is a game my husband, Jason, and I love to play. Whenever we get some time away just the two of us, we settle into a familiar rhythm of asking each other about likes and dislikes, pet peeves, and dreams for the future. We've been married so long we already know the answers to most of the questions. But we keep asking them because every question is like a love note that says, "I know you."

Jason was my high school sweetheart. Two decades later, he knows me better than anyone else on the planet. He can order for me at restaurants because he already knows what I like. He can read the expressions on my face without me ever saying a word. *Sigh.* Romantic, isn't it?

Knowing and being known is a beautiful gift, and it's what transforms Hagar's story from a story of rejection and hurt to a story of acceptance and purpose.

> Picture the person who knows you best. Perhaps it's your mom, your best friend, or your sister. Write his or her name here _____.

If possible, send that person a text and ask the following questions:

1. How many hairs are on my head?

2. How many years will I live?

3. What sentence am I going to say next? (Make them guess before you say it.)

How many did they answer correctly? Zero, right? Don't worry, that doesn't mean your best friend isn't truly your best friend or that your mom secretly adopted you. It just means they aren't the foremost experts on you. There is One who knows you better than your parents or friends. He even knows you better than you know yourself. We find His name in Hagar's story.

Let's revisit Genesis 16:13.

> *So she named the LORD who spoke to her: "You are El-roi,"*
> *for she said, "In this place, have I actually seen the one who*
> *sees me?"*

Hagar named the Lord "a God of seeing" (ESV). That's a weird name, right? It's like calling me a "woman of writing" or you a "player of basketball," but this was all Hagar knew of the character of God. She didn't grow up going to Sunday school; she'd never attended a church service. She didn't know how she was *supposed* to talk about God; she just knew that when no one else saw her, He did.

Some Bible scholars translate Hagar's description of God as *El Roi*. *El* is the Hebrew name for God meaning "majesty or power."[1] *Roi* translates looking, seeing, or sight.[2] Hagar was declaring that seeing her was not just something God *did*, but who He *is*. Knowing she was seen helped her tap into the Lord's strength and face her difficult circumstances.

Why do you think being seen was so significant to her?

Hagar's mistress, Sarai, didn't know her. She saw Hagar as property, not a person. Cast out in the desert, Hagar must have felt utterly alone. Hagar's husband, Abram, didn't know her. He didn't choose her. He didn't propose to her. He didn't pursue her. He used her as a means to get what he wanted (a child and a happy wife).

Describe a time when you felt alone, like no one really saw or knew you.

Another way to describe being seen is being known. Hagar faced difficult circumstances. She was forced to marry a man she likely did not love. She was pregnant with a child she'd have to share with her mistress. She was hated by the woman in charge of her care, and ultimately she was cast out alone into the desert. Hagar's story is no fairy tale. But that's the lower story, remember? There's a higher, more significant plotline at play. Hagar's life reveals a critical piece of the puzzle of who God is.

He is a God who sees us. He is a God who knows us.

Let's circle back to those questions you asked of the person who knows you best. They weren't trick questions. It's possible to find an answer for each one of them. Let me show you.

Q. *How many hairs are on your head?* Your hairdresser doesn't know the answer. You don't even know the answer, but God does.

> Write out Matthew 10:30.

God has numbered the hairs on your head. Not a single strand falls out or gets stuck in your hairbrush without Him knowing about it. Amazing, right?

Q. *How many years will I live?* If you could crack that code, you'd be a rich girl. We'd all like to know exactly how many days we'll have on the planet, but crystal balls don't really work and we can't see into the future. But God can.

> Write out Psalm 139:16.

Park on this truth for a moment. Let it sink deep into your heart: *Before you drew your very first breath, God saw your last.*

Q. *What sentence am I going to say next?* Write out a sentence. It can be something profound or something silly or something random.

> Ready, set, write!

> Now, write out Psalm 139:4.

Before you ever speak (or write) a word, God knows what you're going to say. He knows the hairs on your head and the days of your life. He knows your hopes and your dreams, your fears and your failures. *God knows you better than you know you.*

Let's look at Genesis 16:13 one more time. First Hagar declared, "You are a God of seeing" (ESV). Then she said, "truly I have seen him who looks after me" (ESV). First, God saw Hagar and suddenly Hagar could see God. Once we acknowledge the truth that God sees our lives from start to finish, we are suddenly aware of how well He knows us. Knowing and being known by my husband certainly makes my heart flutter, but it doesn't compare to the beautiful truth that I am known by the same God who placed the stars in the sky. Even more amazing, He invites us to know Him too.

I'm afraid we've been singing the song all wrong since childhood. Jesus loves us this I know, but Jesus knows us, this I *love*!

Hagar's circumstances didn't change. The angel commanded her to go back to her difficult home life and face what awaited her there. She found the strength to do it because she encountered a God who saw it all. You can face your life circumstances knowing nothing slides past God or escapes Him. He is truly the God who sees you.

TALK ABOUT IT

Discuss the following questions with your group.

> Do you relate more to Hagar or Sarai in this story? Why?
>
> Why did Hagar chose to go back to her home rather than staying in the desert?
>
> Why do all humans have a craving to be known?

THINK ABOUT IT

I affectionately call Psalm 139 the *knowing* Psalm because for 24 verses the Psalmist described how intimately the Lord knows each of us.

> Read through the entire Psalm. As you read, list all the things God knows about you.

) *Who? Hope For the Left Out*

Hagar's story is the only place in Scripture where God is called *El Roi*, but the story of God knowing and desiring to be known by His people is written onto every page of the Bible. Today, we're going to complete two bonus Story I.D. charts.

LEAH

Leah's story is found just a few pages after Hagar's in Genesis 29–30. Leah is the wife of Jacob, the great-grandson of Hagar's husband, Abraham.

THE WIDOW OF NAIN

The widow of Nain's story is found in the New Testament in Luke 7:11-17, thousands of years after God's encounter with Hagar in the desert. See if you can figure out what these women have in common.

Read Leah's story in Genesis 29–30. Fill in the following Story I.D. chart.

Who   Leah
_____

What
_____

When
_____

Where
_____

Why

Read the story of the Widow of Nain found in Luke 7:11-17. The Bible doesn't tell us her name, but God knows it. He is the God who sees, after all! What do you discover about this woman's life from the text?

Who   The Widow of Nain
_____

What
_____

When
_____

Where
_____

Why

Hagar was a young slave girl, pregnant and hated by her mistress. Leah shared a husband with her sister. The widow's only son died. All three of these women's stories are branded with heartache, but there is another thread that ties these women together. They were each rejected, left out, or cast aside. These women were not popular. We don't see them being treasured and adored by friends or family. They weren't the center of positive attention. Instead they were rejected and abandoned. Yet God saw each of them. He found Hagar cast out in the desert. He saw Leah in her lonely marriage. He reached out to the widow of Nain as she followed her son's casket.

If you've ever felt left out, abandoned, rejected, or cast aside, then you have this promise to cling to: *God sees you. He knows you.*

In Isaiah 49:13-16 we find a beautiful promise from God. Read the passage and highlight verse 14.

Zion is a symbol for God's people. While Hagar named God "a God of seeing" in Genesis 16:13, His people had a different perception of Him in this verse. What name do you think they would give Him based on verse 14?

God's people felt rejected, forsaken, and forgotten. Have you ever felt like God has forgotten you? Read the passage again and circle the ways the Lord responded to His people.

Our feelings may scream that God has forgotten us, but feelings aren't facts. The promise we have in Scripture is that God loves to comfort His people (v. 13). He has compassion on us (v. 13). Even though a mom can forget the baby she holds on her lap, God will never, ever forget us (v. 15). He has tattooed our names on the palm of His hand (v. 16).

Choose one of the women from today's study and write her a note of encouragement. Tell her why she can have hope, even when others reject her. Be sure to include a Bible verse or two.

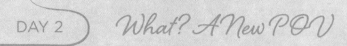

What? A New POV

Remember how at the beginning of this chapter we looked at Genesis 16 from two different points of view (POV)? First, we read the story through Sarai's eyes and then through Hagar's. That's a good exercise for helping us dig deeply into a Biblical narrative, but we don't want to get stuck on the lower story. The most important point of view is God's.

Psalm 33:13-15 describes God's unique perspective. Check it out.

> In your Bible, identify where God looks at us from. Highlight what God sees.

God watches us from His throne in heaven. If you've ever flown on a plane, you know that altitude changes your perspective drastically. Now imagine seeing the world not from the seat of an airplane, but from the seat in the throne room of heaven. This is God's unique perspective of your life and the lives of everyone around you.

We tend to see our lives in extreme close up. It can be difficult to look past the worries, fears, excitement, and challenges of each day. But God sees our lives from a much higher vantage point. One word used to describe God's POV is *omniscience*. He is uniquely able to see and know everything all the time.

> What three things about your life are you glad God sees?
>
> 1.
>
> 2.
>
> 3.
>
> What are three things about your life you wish God couldn't see?

When we revisit Genesis 16 with God's omniscience in mind, we can suddenly see the higher story. He saw Sarai's infertility and Hagar's pregnancy. He saw the way Sarai treated Hagar with contempt and the way Hagar responded in hurt. He saw the future of Abraham's family from the beginning until the end of time. The people in this story were only able to see what was right in front of their faces, but from His throne in heaven God saw the bigger story.

This is just one reason God is worthy of our trust. He sees what we cannot see. He knows what we cannot know. And He has promised to work every detail of our lives for our good and His glory (Rom. 8:28).

How might Sarai have responded differently to her circumstances if she focused on the fact that God saw her, knew her, and loved her?

How might these truths have impacted Hagar's thoughts and actions?

HOPE IN THE ONE WHO HANGS THE STARS

When I face difficult circumstances, I often pray, "You call the stars out one by one and not one of them is missing. I trust that you can handle this."

It's my way of saying: "I know you see this. I know you're in control. I trust you with this." It's a prayer that brings me tremendous peace and comfort whenever I face something tough. I borrowed it from Isaiah 40, a passage the declares God's mighty omniscience. Look at verse 26:

"Look up and see!
Who created these?
He brings out the stars by number;
he calls all of them by name.
Because of his great power and strength,
not one of them is missing.

As you close your study today, spend some time reading through Isaiah 40. Highlight examples of God's unique POV in the text. Then, fill in the following prayer.

Lord, you call the stars out one by one and not one of them is missing. I trust that you can handle _____ (fill in the blank with whatever is worrying you today). Amen.

DAY 3

When?
Past, Present, and Future.

If you could time travel to any date on the calendar, which date would you pick?

Did you select the signing of the Declaration of Independence in 1776? Or the day your parents were married? How about the moment smart phones were invented?

Consider this: *God was there for each of those moments in history.* He's seen every wedding ever performed, watched every birth, and viewed every war and the signing of every peace treaty. He has seen every second of your life so far and already knows how the rest of your story will be written. We see this clearly in Hagar's story.

In Genesis 16:8, an angel of the Lord said to Hagar, "Hagar, servant of Sarai, where have you come from and where are you going?" (ESV).

Do you think the angel knew the answers to his own questions? Why or why not?

Now, think like a journalist and revisit the verse again. What do you see? How did the angel address Hagar?

The angel said, "Hagar, servant of Sarai, …" yet Hagar had not spoken. The angel initiated this conversation, and he already knew Hagar's name and her position within the house of Abraham and Sarai. Think of that a different way: God saw Hagar's past.

Yes, Hagar was the biological child of earthly parents, but think back to the *Imago Dei* found in Genesis 1:27. Who is Hagar's creator? God is. The promise of Psalm 139:13 is that God knit Hagar together in her mother's womb. Before anyone else ever saw her face, God saw her.

The good and the bad, the happy and the hurtful, the godly decisions and the sinful ones—God sees them all. And yet, there is nothing in our past that keeps God from pursuing us in our present. God meets Hagar in her current struggle. He comes to her as she sits in the desert. He sees you right now. His presence is available to you every single moment.

God also saw Hagar's future. Look at Genesis 16:10-12. What specific predictions did the angel make about Hagar's future?

When Hagar declared God "a God of seeing" (Gen. 16:3, ESV), she knew He didn't only see this one moment in time. He saw everything that had ever happened to her and everything that would ever happen to her. He saw her unborn baby and knew what he would be like as a man. He saw the future of her family throughout the generations. God saw the bigger picture. He knew the higher story.

Read the following verses. List what each one teaches us about God's relationship to time.

Psalm 90:4

Psalm 102:12

2 Peter 3:8

Our God is an everlasting God. He has no beginning. He will have no end. He is an eternal God. He will rule and reign forever. While He created time, He is not bound with it like we are. What feels like years to us, feels like a moment to Him. This is the higher story.

For as heaven is higher than earth, so my ways are higher than your ways, and my thoughts than your thoughts.
ISAIAH 55:9

Sketch a picture that illustrates the truth found in Isaiah 55:9.

DAY 4 — *The Bigger Story*

Is it possible that Hagar's story is really a story about the gospel? Let's look again and find out.

Read Galatians 4:21-30.

These words were written by Paul after Christ's time on earth. Paul knew the lower story. He was aware of the details of Hagar and Sarai's lives, but he didn't park there. He looked for the higher story, the gospel story.

Paul used Hagar and Sarai as symbols to describe a bigger truth, comparing them to two covenants. Hagar represents one *covenant*, or *promise from God*, and Sarai represents a second covenant.

Fill in the details about each covenant below.

Hagar's Covenant	Sarai's Covenant

Hagar's tragic story represents life without Christ. She was enslaved to sin and destined to pass that along to the next generation. This is our position without Christ.

What does Romans 6:20 remind us to consider?

What did Jesus declare in John 8:34?

Hagar's life illustrated the hopelessness of this truth. She was a slave, bound to her masters. Scripture doesn't give us any indication she ever experienced freedom.

In contrast, Sarai's story showcases the covenant of freedom. God's promise to us is that, when we surrender our lives to Him and turn from our sin, we experience true freedom. We were born as slaves to sin, but because of Jesus our chains are removed and we are adopted as children of the promise.

At first glance, Genesis 16 looks like a story about a pregnant slave girl in the desert. When we look again, we see it is so much more! Hagar's life declares who God is.

There's power in declaring the truths we find in Scripture. It helps God's Word move from our heads to our hearts and then overflow into our lives.

Declare God's truth by writing out the following sentence several times: *I am not a slave to sin. I am a child of the promise.*

Take the message a step further by sending it out as a social media post.

God Rescues: A Beautiful Song

Miriam sang to them:
Sing to the Lord,
for he is highly exalted;
he has thrown the horse
and its rider into the sea.
EXODUS 15:21

STRETCH

Miriam's story began long before she was born. Let me show you what I mean.

Read Exodus 6:16-20.

I'm guessing I lost you at Gershon. It can be tempting to skip or skim the genealogies found in the Bible, but as you grow as a student of God's Word and learn to approach Scripture as the source of truth, I hope you will pay closer attention to the genealogies. Here are three reasons why.

1. EVERY WORD MATTERS.

Fill in the blanks for 2 Timothy 3:16.

_____ Scripture is _____ by _____ and is
_____ for _____, for _____,
for _____, for _____ in _____.

From the first word in Genesis to the last word in Revelation, every section of Scripture is God-given and useful in helping us understand the character of God and living like He calls us to live. That includes the genealogies.

2. EVERY WORD OF GOD PROVES TRUE.

An easy way to prove the truth found in Scripture is through the genealogies.

Isaiah 11:1 declares this promise:

> *Then a shoot will grow from the stump of Jesse, and a branch from his roots will bear fruit.*

That promise wouldn't amount to much without the genealogy found in Matthew 1:1–17 and again in Luke 3:23–38. Go ahead and look them up.

This list starts with Abraham and ends with Jesus' birth. Smack dab in the middle we find a gem. Write out Matthew 1:6 below.

The branch Isaiah wrote about was Jesus. His words were written around 700 years before Christ was born. If we skipped this genealogy, we would miss the wonder of seeing this prophecy fulfilled.

3. GOD CARES ABOUT ALL PEOPLE.

We don't know much about the individuals whose names are listed in Exodus 6:16-20. We would struggle to fill out anything more than a name on a Story I.D. chart for each one. And yet, as we learned in our last session, God is the foremost expert on each person on the list.

Miriam isn't even listed in this genealogy, but as we dig into her story, we will trace her beginnings back to this spot.

STORY I.D.

Use the following verses to fill in the chart for Miriam. These verses will just provide some basic information about Miriam. We will dig deeper into her story together and you can add details to this chart as we go.

- Exodus 15:20-21
- Numbers 20:1
- Numbers 26:59
- 1 Chronicles 6:3

Who   Miriam

What

When

Where

Why

DIGGING DEEPER

Miriam is one of very few people in Scripture whose story we get to see from beginning to end. We find her parents' names in Numbers 26:59, and we find her brothers' names in Exodus 6:20 and 1 Chronicles 6:3.

If you have a sibling whose shadow you always seem to be stuck in, you can likely relate to Miriam. She is the sister of the most famous Old Testament prophet of all times, Moses.

List what you already know about Moses' story.

If you could sum up the theme of Moses' story in just one word, what word would it be? I'd choose the word *deliverance*.

- He was *delivered* from the river as a baby.
- He was *delivered* from the desert by a burning bush.
- He was *delivered* from the Egyptians through a series of miracles.
- He *delivered* God's people into the promised land.

Miriam's story is forever tethered to her brother's. Hers is a story about deliverance too. Some of the details are the same. Some are different. One cord that binds these siblings together also connects them to us. We all need a deliverer.

Write out Psalm 18:2.

Deliverer is just one word the psalmist used here to describe God. In the following chart, fill in the other descriptions of God we find in this verse.

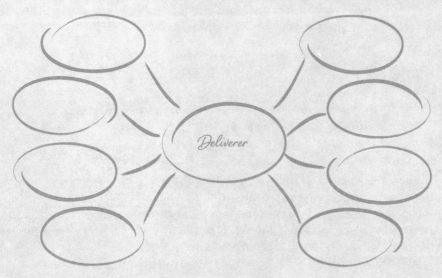

Another word for a *deliverer* is *rescuer* or *savior*. Miriam's story helps us see that we serve a God who rescues and saves.

HE RESCUED HER FAMILY

We catch our first glimpses of Miriam as a girl, wading beside the river.

Read Exodus 1:6-2:10.

This is the beginning of Moses' story. That is one POV through which we can view these verses, but it is also the beginning of Miriam's story. She is the sister on the bank waiting to see what would become of her brother. She was older than Moses and spared from the Pharaoh's wicked edict of death because she was a girl, but she grew up in difficult times.

Circle back to Exodus 1:6-22. Describe what life was like for Miriam and her family.

Her people were enslaved. A wicked ruler mandated that all boy babies must be killed, and the brother she had spent three months getting to know and love was floating down the river in a basket toward an unknown future. These were not easy circumstances for Miriam and her family.

Journal about a time when your family faced difficult circumstances. What emotions did you experience during that time that Miriam might have experienced as well?

Despite her swirling emotions, Miriam made a bold move. What did she do in Exodus 2:7-8?

It's possible Miriam was motivated by fear or naivety, but I somehow doubt either was the force behind her actions. Miriam was a Hebrew. Her people worshiped *Yahweh*, the same God we serve. She'd likely heard stories of how God delivered Noah's family, Abraham's family, and Joseph's family. She'd probably been told about God's promise to create a great nation through Abraham. Instead of seeing her brother through the lens of her feelings or circumstances, she looked at him through the eyes of faith.

What do you struggle to trust God with? Are there any circumstances, relationships, or needs that feel like they are thrown into a basket floating toward an unknown future?

HE RESCUED HER PEOPLE

We find Miriam on the banks of another river in Exodus 15.

Read Exodus 15:1-21.

Nearly 80 years had passed between Moses' birth and adoption and this moment. So much had happened! Moses, Miriam, and Aaron grew up.

Complete the following timeline.

Date	Scripture Passage	Description
1486 BC	Exodus 2:11-15	
1446 BC	Exodus 2:23-25	
1446 BC	Exodus 3:1-8	God called Moses from a burning bush.
1446 BC	Exodus 7–12	God sent ten plagues to afflict Egypt.
1446 BC	Exodus 12:29-32	
1446 BC	Exodus 14:5-31	

Sure, Moses' rescue from the river as a baby was dramatic, but this was a showstopper! Miriam's people were being chased by an army of chariots led by an enraged ruler. They had nowhere to turn and no way to save themselves, but God intervened.

> Look up Exodus 15:20-21. Miriam watched her enemies drown and her people were miraculously saved. How did she respond?

Miriam shows us that worship is the right response to God's deliverance. You don't have to have rhythm or a superstar voice to praise God for all He has saved you from. Miriam simply grabbed her tambourine and declared what God had done.

> As you end your time together, listen to a worship song and take some time to praise God for being your deliverer.

HE SAVED HER

Maybe the idea of Jesus as your Savior feels a bit impersonal. You know He cares about His people as a whole, but it's tough to imagine He cares about you. Maybe you think He's too wrapped up in the "big stuff" like wars, famine, and global politics to have time to deliver you from the worries you face today. Miriam's story teaches a different truth.

In Numbers 12, we find a high stakes sibling quarrel. Read the chapter and answer the following questions:

Why were Miriam and Aaron annoyed with Moses (vv. 1-2)?

Why was God angry with Miriam and Aaron (vv. 6-9)?

What punishment did Miriam receive for speaking against her brother (vv. 10,13-15)?

Imagine what would happen if the next time you had an argument with a sibling, you were struck with a devastating disease and exiled from your home. That is exactly what happened to Miriam. God was Moses' defender in this passage, intervening when his siblings questioned his leadership, but Moses also defended Miriam. She was guilty, yet God rescued her from her punishment. He did not leave her in her diseased state. He did not force her to live outside of the camp forever.

Read Psalm 40:17, and answer the following questions:

What happens when you try to be your own defender/savior?

What has God already saved you from?

What do you need to trust Him to rescue you from today?

TALK ABOUT IT

Discuss the following questions with your group.

What do you see as the defining moment of Miriam's life?

How does Miriam's story point to the bigger story of who God is?

How does it change our response to conflict and trial to know that we are not our own defenders, but God is?

THINK ABOUT IT

Think back to the definition of the gospel we explored in Session 1. Here it is for review:

The gospel:

* We are sinners.

* Christ is our Savior.

* Only through Him are we released from the punishment of sin and free to spend eternity with our Creator.

How does Miriam's story illustrate the truth of the gospel? Compare notes with other members of your group.

DAY 1) *Who? Those Who Feared God*

I'm sending you on a scavenger hunt! Find two names hidden in Miriam's story.

Shiphrah   *Puah*

You can look for them in the passages we've already read or use a Bible concordance or online resource like Bible Gateway.

Shiphrah and Puah were the midwives who disobeyed Pharaoh's orders and let the Hebrew babies live. Read Exodus 1:15-21 and fill out a Story I.D. chart for these women.

Who   Shiphrah and Puah

What

When

Where

Why

Pharaoh was the most powerful man in Egypt. These women were not government leaders. They weren't political movers and shakers. They were midwives who dared to defy Pharaoh's orders. These women feared God more than they feared Pharaoh. They were more concerned with God's will than the will of those who seemed to hold all the power in their world.

Read the following verses and list common ideas you see in each of them.

> Job 28:28
> Proverbs 1:7
> Proverbs 14:26
> Proverbs 33:8

These verses aren't encouraging us to approach God like we would a scary movie, but to respond to God with honor and respect. We are to value His Word and seek His approval more than man's.

You can also think of the fear of man as placing too much value on what others think. While it is wise to honor others, it is unwise to let others' opinions determine your actions or perceived value. The Bible calls this a *snare*, or a *trap*—it holds us back from living like God has called us to live.

Consider the following areas of your life. In each area, indicate whether you're more concerned about what God thinks or what people think.

- My social media page(s):

    What God thinks   What people think

- How I dress:

    What God thinks   What people think

- My entertainment choices:

    What God thinks   What people think

Our tendency is to cater to others' expectations. This might have seemed like the smoother path for Shiphrah and Puah, but they chose to obey God instead of man. This story is filled with individuals who feared God more than they feared man, who refused to get trapped by people's expectations.

Read Proverbs 29:25 and then rewrite Miriam's story with this in mind.

What would have happened if Miriam's parents had feared man rather than God?

What would have happened if Shiphrah and Puah had feared man rather than God?

When we fear God more than man, we are free to follow His plans for our lives. We are untangled from the pressure to impress others and free to live our lives in service to our King.

Journal a prayer asking the Lord to help you value His commands above all. Confess areas where you tend to value man's opinion over God's Word and ask Him to help you avoid the trap of the fear of man.

What? The Makings of a Great Leader

Make a list of the greatest leaders of all times. I've listed two names to get you started.

Napoleon

George Washington

History champions leaders who are bold, charismatic, and sometimes ruthless. Moses' story helps us see that God is looking for a different set of qualities for leadership.

Look up the following verses. Next to each verse, list a character trait you see in Moses (ex. humble).

Exodus 2:6

Exodus 4:2-5

Exodus 4:10

Exodus 15:1-2

Numbers 12:3-8

Did you write down characteristics like timid, obedient, and meek? These aren't qualities that are likely to show up in profiles of the movers and shakers of our culture, yet God used Moses to lead a movement so significant we're still talking about it more than 3,000 years later! Often, the way things work in the kingdom of God is opposite of the way they work in our world.

First Corinthians 1:27 says it this way:

> Instead, God has chosen what is foolish in the world to shame the wise, and God has chosen what is weak in the world to shame the strong.

Rewrite this verse in your own words. What do you think God's point is?

God often takes what we think we know and flips it upside down. Let me show you. Based on what you've learned in this session and what you've learned elsewhere about Moses, circle the statements that are true about Moses.

He is the son of slaves.

He was adopted as a baby.

He was a general in Pharaoh's army.

He killed a man.

He was a fugitive from the law.

He married a woman who was a different nationality than him.

He was a shepherd.

He had a speech impediment.

The people always listened to him and respected him.

Moses never served as a general in his adopted grandpa's army, and the people didn't always listen to him. The reality of who he was is much less impressive from a human perspective. If Moses were up for election, few of us would vote for him. Fortunately, God doesn't call us to serve based on the popular vote.

We can't assume we know all of the reasons God chose Moses, but we do know that God clearly values and desires to use humble servants.

Read Luke 22:25-27.

Moses was a man who led like Jesus, a humble servant.

List the areas of leadership in your own life.

Consider this: *Am I trying to lead like the world, through power and popularity, or am I trying to lead like Christ, through humble service?*

Pray and ask the Holy Spirit to help you see areas where you need to be shaped more into His image as you lead.

When?
Under an Edict of Death

Revisit Exodus 1:8–2:10 and list any details that stick out to you.

We aren't told the name of the oppressive Pharaoh in power at the time of Moses' birth. Pharaoh was not his name, but his title, much like our term *president*. Many of the details of his life have been wiped from the pages of history completely, but we do know what type of ruler he was.

Look back at Exodus 1:8-13. What words would you use to describe this man?

Motivated by fear (v. 9), Pharaoh set out to make life miserable for the Israelites, vowing to "deal shrewdly" (v. 10) with them.

What specific ways did Pharaoh mistreat God's people in each of the following verses?

Exodus 1:11

Exodus 1:13

Exodus 1:15-16

When forced labor, slavery, and harsh working conditions didn't work, Pharaoh resorted to a different, more desperate attempt to control God's people. He commanded that all of the boy babies be hurled into the Nile River. Scripture has already informed us that the Israelites had become a significant people group. We don't know exactly how many Israelites lived in Egypt during this time, but Exodus 12:37 does give us a clue to the scope of their size.

According to this verse, how many Israelite men participated in the exodus?

If half of those men had female counterparts, the count would be up to 900,000 people. Now think about what would happen if two-thirds of those people had three children each—that increases the number to almost 1.5 million! That's close to the entire population of Philadelphia, Pennsylvania!

Moses was born under an edict of death. Based on the circumstances, he shouldn't have taken a first breath, yet he lived to lead numerous Israelites to freedom. One of the lessons Moses' life teaches is that man cannot stop God's plans.

Read Isaiah 14:24-27. Highlight any variation of the words purpose or plan.

Now, look at the ways something happens if God plans it:

- "so it will be" (v. 24)
- "so it will happen" (v. 24)
- "who can stand in its way?" (v. 27)
- "who can turn it back?" (v. 27)

Write this sentence in your notes: *Nothing can stop the plans of God*.

Moses was born under an edict of death, yet he lived a long, fruitful life. The Israelites were enslaved under a wicked ruler, yet they were free to leave their bonds of slavery behind. Miriam looked forward and saw a raging sea and behind she saw a raging army, yet she found herself singing for joy on the other side of it all.

God's plan for your life can't be stopped. What is His plan exactly? I can't wait to show you tomorrow!

The Bigger Story

Just like Moses, Jesus was born under an edict of death.

Grab your Bible and read Matthew 2:1-18.

More than a thousand years had passed since Moses' birth. Jesus, our Savior, had just been born in Bethlehem when Herod did something unthinkable.

Write out Matthew 2:16.

Sound familiar?

Pharaoh tried to stop God's people by killing their baby boys. Herod tried to stop God Himself by doing the same. But what have we already learned about the plans of God?

Let's look for other similarities between the birth of Jesus and the birth of Moses. To find some of these answers you'll need to flip back to Matthew 1 and pay close attention to the genealogy.

What nationality were Moses' parents?	What nationality were Jesus' parents?
Were Moses' parents likely rich or poor?	Were Jesus' parents likely rich or poor?
Where was Moses born?	Where was Jesus born?
Who was in power when Moses was born?	Who was in power when Jesus was born?

There are many ways these two stories intersect. Moses was born in Egypt under an edict of death, yet he fled to the promised land. God used him to deliver numerous people from slavery in Egypt. Even though the number seems pretty huge, that's the lower story.

> Write out John 3:16. (*Bonus: See if you can write the verse from memory and then double check your answer in God's Word.*)

> Who did God send Jesus to save?

Jesus was born in the promised land under an edict of death, yet fled to Egypt. God used Him to deliver all of His people from bondage to sin, death, and darkness. Herod was only the first in a long line of rulers who tried to stop Jesus, but nothing can stop the plans of God. Moses' and Miriam's story of deliverance is a beautiful foreshadowing of the gospel.

> As you close this session, meditate on Romans 6:6-8, thanking Jesus for freeing you from slavery to sin so you can live with Him in the promised land of heaven.

God Inspires: A Beautiful Trust

*Then Deborah said to Barak, "Go! This is the
day the LORD has handed Sisera over to you.
Hasn't the LORD gone before you?"*
JUDGES 4:14a

STRETCH

Let's kick off this session with a big word that describes an important tool
for understanding God's Word: *Hermeneutics*. This is a fancy word for
a relatively simple concept. The dictionary gives us this definition: "the
study of the methodological principles of interpretation (as of the Bible)."[1]

Highlight *methodological, interpretation*, and *Bible*. Imagine we threw those
words into a hat and jumbled them around. If we pulled them out one by
one and reassembled them, then we might get this definition: Hermeneutics
is a method (let's just drop the "ological" business) of interpreting the Bible.

What's the difference between reading and interpreting?

We read to find information and interpret to understand or apply it.

Write out 2 Timothy 2:15.

How does this verse ask us to handle the Word of God?

We don't want to mishandle the Word of God, right? To help us with that,
here are three of the guidelines of hermeneutics.

1. THE BIBLE IS INTERPRETED LITERALLY.

Grab a dictionary or use one on your phone and look up the words *literally* and *figuratively* to compare the definitions.

> Literally means...

> Figuratively means...

In other words:

1. We read the events in Scripture as actual historical events, not fairy tales.

2. We assume God means what He says in each verse rather than digging for a secret, hidden meaning.

2. WE LOOK FOR CULTURAL CLUES.

As much as possible, shift your POV to see the text as the original audience did rather than only looking at it through our own modern lens. The Bible can never mean anything for us that it did not mean to the people at the time it was written.

3. SEE SCRIPTURE AS THE EXPERT.

Commentaries can be a great tool, as can sermons and books about the Bible, but those resources are all just supplements to interpreting God's Word. If you want to understand God's Word, read it carefully and often. You will be amazed at what God will show you!

These tools will help you as we dig in to the intriguing (and sometimes strange) story of Deborah. Before we start, let's take a minute to ask the Lord to help us to handle His Word correctly.

STORY I.D.

Chart Deborah's story found in Judges 4-5.

Who   Deborah

What

When

Where

Why

DIGGING DEEPER

Deborah was a judge and prophetess. Those aren't titles we use often anymore. Let's do a little digging to figure out what they mean.

Summarize Judges 2:16.

Judges like Deborah weren't selected by the president and approved by the Senate like our Supreme Court Justices. They had divine appointments. They were handpicked by God.

The "them" in this verse refers to God's people. But what (or who) exactly did they need saving from? Let's look for the higher story by retracing our steps through the profiles we've already tackled in this study. What major events have shaped God's people so far?

Fill in the timeline with details we've learned from the lives of Eve, Hagar, and Miriam.

God created man and woman _____ His _____ (Gen. 1:27).

God promised He would build a great nation through _____ and his wife, _____ (Gen. 12:1-2,5).

God used _____ to lead His people out of slavery (Ex. 12:31-32). That period is known as the exodus.

Because of _____, Adam and Eve were cast out of the garden and separated from _____ (Gen. 3:22-24).

Abram and Sarai tried to fast track God's timing by gaining an heir through Sarai's servant, _____ (Gen. 16:1-3). That child's name was _____ (Gen. 16:11).

God kept His promise to Abraham, and God's people grew and grew. Pharaoh, the ruler of _____, feared their numbers and forced them to live as _____ (Ex. 1:8-14).

By investigating the lives of just three women, we're able to see more than a thousand years of human history and God's clear hand in it all. Let's fill in a few gaps between the moment when Miriam celebrated her people's deliverance and God rallied judges to rescue His people (again). Many details are left out, but here are some highlights.

- Moses was given the Ten Commandments (Ex. 20:1-21).
- God's people wandered in the desert for 40 years (Josh. 5:6).
- Moses died and was succeeded by Joshua (Deut. 34:1-8; Josh. 1:1).
- God's people drove out some of their enemies in the promised land (Josh. 1–24).

Read Judges 2:11-15. What themes do you see in the history of God's people?

How does the last sentence of verse 15 describe them?

Once again God's people were enslaved and separated from the God who made them in His image.

Enter Deborah. While God's people failed and flailed, Deborah sat beneath a palm tree and called them to do right. She was a wife, maybe a mother, a warrior, and a poetess. It's tough not to like a woman that strong and brave, but what I love most about Deborah is the way she championed others.

Look back at Judges 4:1-7. Fill in any details you missed from this passage in the "what" section of your Story I.D. chart.

God's people were enslaved by a wicked ruler. Sound familiar? That's the lower story. Force your eyes to look at the higher story. In what ways was God at work?

God asked Barak to lead a rebellion against Jabin and Sisera. He promised Barak the victory, yet Barak hadn't taken a single step toward his enemy. Deborah called him to her palm tree court and reminded him *who* he was, or more accurately, she reminded him *whose* he was. He bore the image of the God of the universe. Since he had been handpicked by God, he could not fail. Deborah didn't look Barak in the eye and imply "you can do this." Instead, she reminded him, "God can do this!"

This helps us understand her titles of *judge* and *prophetess*.

- A judge is someone who hears evidence and determines a righteous course of action.
- A prophetess (or prophet) is someone who publicly declares a message from the Lord.

How do you see Deborah acting as judge in this story?

How do you see her acting as a prophetess?

A BEAUTIFUL CHAMPION

When you hear the word "champion" what comes to mind?

In the church, a victory secured by any one of us should be celebrated by all of us. Like Deborah did for Barak, God asks us to cheer for each other. In 1 Corinthians 12:26, Paul said it this way:

> *So if one member suffers, all the members suffer with it; if one member is honored, all the members rejoice with it.*

Deborah knew that Barak's victory was her victory. If he would trust God's promises and go to war with the pagan king, all of God's people would ultimately win.

After her words to Barak in Judges 4:14, what happened in Judges 4:16?

Jabin's army was decimated. Sisera escaped only to be killed with a tent peg. That victory freed God's people from their slavery to Jabin.

According to Judges 5:31, how long did God's people enjoy peace?

How might Deborah's story have played out differently if she had criticized Barak rather than cheering him on?

I love Deborah's story because she understood a secret I've missed for most of my life: When the people around me trust God and obey Him, that's good for me. It gives health to the body of Christ that I am a part of. In the same way, when God's people disobey God, ignore His promises, or refuse to deal with sin, that's bad for me. It poisons the body that I'm connected to. In some ways, God calls each of us to the roles of judge and prophetess. We are to lovingly point our Christian brothers and sisters toward God's Word, and we all need to declare God's promises often. When that calling seems impossible, it helps to remember that Deborah's trust wasn't ultimately in Barak. He was a reluctant and needy leader.

Instead, Deborah trusted God. She knew God would come through, even when Barak hesitated. She knew this was the God who speaks, the God who sees, and the God who rescues. God had a long history of responding to His people. Deborah simply trusted that He would do it again. She used her influence to remind others of God's character. She cheered for others. She celebrated others. She championed others.

TALK ABOUT IT

Discuss the following questions with your group.

Read through Paul's words in 1 Corinthians 12:26 again. How have you seen this played out practically?

When you do not encourage other Christians to obey the Lord, what does that reveal about your trust in Him?

How can you champion or cheer for your fellow Christians more often?

THINK ABOUT IT

Do you have a Deborah in your life? Someone who calls you to live according to God's truth, reminds you who you are in Him, and nudges you to live like He has called you to live? Take a moment to write that person a thank you note now.

DAY 1 — *Who? Life-givers!*

Have you ever heard the saying,

> *Sticks and stones may break my bones, but words will never hurt me?*

This hasn't been true in my life. The Bible warns us that "death and life are in the power of the tongue" (Prov. 18:21a). Words have power—we can use them to build others up or to tear them down.

Match the following Proverbs about our words with the correct reference.

Proverbs 11:9	Pleasant words are a honeycomb: sweet to the taste and health to the body.
Proverbs 11:17	There is gold and a multitude of jewels, but knowledgeable lips are a rare treasure.
Proverbs 15:1	A kind man benefits himself, but a cruel person brings ruin on himself.
Proverbs 16:24	With his mouth the ungodly destroys his neighbor, but through knowledge the righteous are rescued.
Proverbs 25:18	A gentle answer turns away anger, but a harsh word stirs up wrath.
Proverbs 20:15	A person giving false testimony against his neighbor is like a club, a sword, or a sharp arrow.

Our words might not literally break bones or kill someone, but they do have the power to encourage or discourage, to give life and hope to others, or to cause sorrow and despair.

Deborah used her words to champion others and to encourage the people around her to trust God. God's people thrived as a result. But what happens when we use our words to tear down instead of to build up?

DESIGNED TO BE LIFE-GIVERS

Circle back to Eve's story and read Genesis 3:20.

Who named Eve? Why did he give her this name specifically?

Some Bible scholars translate Eve's name as "life-producer."[2] Adam and Eve didn't have children yet. He had no frame of reference for how a woman could physically give life as a mother, yet Adam still declared her a life-giver. Eve's name reminds us that one of the ways we bear God's image is by speaking life-giving words, not words that tear down and cause harm.

Journal about a time when someone spoke life-giving words to you. What difference might it have made if that individual had been critical, cruel, or discouraging instead?

James 3:1-12 reminds us of the power of our words. Highlight the analogies used in this passage to describe the tongue.

This passage is packed full of word pictures to help us understand that the tongue is more than the muscle that rests between our teeth. It is a powerful force either for good or for evil.

How did Deborah use her words for good in Judges 4–5? What was the result?

List some specific ways you can use your words for good this week.

What are some ways you tend to use your words poorly?

Close by writing a prayer to Jesus asking for His help to tame your tongue. We all need His guidance to respond like Deborah with encouraging and life-giving words, rather than with discouraging and hurtful words.

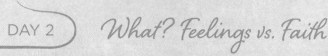

DAY 2) What? Feelings vs. Faith

Quiz time! Answer the following questions:

- I have more bad days than good days.

  Agree   Not Sure   Disagree

- When someone criticizes me, it ruins my whole day.

  Agree   Not Sure   Disagree

- I can't control my emotions when I am stressed.

  Agree   Not Sure   Disagree

- When someone makes me mad, I feel like I need to "vent" or I'll explode.

  Agree   Not Sure   Disagree

- I feel anxious almost daily.

  Agree   Not Sure   Disagree

If you circled mostly "agree," it's possible that you are highly emotionally driven. Your feelings tend to determine the outcome of your day and shift dramatically based on circumstances

If you circled mostly "not sure," ask someone you trust to help you with this quiz. Sometimes it is difficult for us to see how our emotions impact us. Consider their answers carefully.

If you circled mostly "disagree," you still have emotions (we all do) but you haven't put them in the driver's seat of your attitude. That's good! To find out why let's look at Elijah's story.

WHEN GOD WHISPERS

Read 1 Kings 19:9-13.

Elijah's story is nestled in between the stories of Deborah and Job. You'll learn more about him in Session 7. Like Deborah, Elijah was a prophet, assigned to call God's people back to pure worship of the one true God.

The Lord was not in the wind, the earthquake, or the fire. Instead, how did God choose to communicate with Elijah?

We tend to expect God to show up in big ways, but a beautiful by-product of knowing His Word is learning to trust Him even when His voice is as soft as a whisper or when we cannot seem to hear Him at all. Deborah trusted the character and promises of God even when her circumstances roared like a mighty wind all around her.

Circle back to Judges 4:1-3. What was happening in Deborah's world?

Deborah and her people faced an intimidating enemy. It might have felt like God had abandoned them or broken His promise to build a great nation through them, but Deborah did not allow her feelings to determine her actions.

Her trust was not in her circumstances or in her ability to feel God. I have a friend who says it this way, "feelings aren't facts." Another way to state it is *feelings aren't faith*. If our faith is rooted in feelings, we will always be on the lookout for God to show up in grand gestures like earthquakes and fires, and we will miss when He speaks to us through a quiet whisper. We will spend our days anxious, afraid, or angry rather than grabbing onto the peace that flows from trusting God is with us, even when we cannot see or hear Him.

Think of a woman you know who has unshakable faith. How does her trust in God impact her emotions?

When?
Understanding Authority

Circle the words below that best describe your relationship with the authorities in your life (parents, teachers, boss, etc.).

Strained	Annoying	Frustrating
Peaceful	Easy	Fulfilling
Stressful	Tough	

Lean in. Listen closely. I want to tell you a secret: Submitting to authority is tough for everyone.

Whether it's obeying your curfew, meeting your teacher's expectations, or following your boss' orders, submission is tough!

Highlight the names of the women we've studied so far who struggled with authority.

Eve	Hagar	Deborah
Sarai	Miriam	

A NEW TWIST ON AUTHORITY

The Bible has lots to say on the subject of authority. Let's take a look.

Read Romans 13:1-7.

This passage is a treasure trove when it comes to helping us understand how to respond to authority. Let's mine it and dig out some nuggets of truth.

In your Bible, indicate how God instructs us to respond to our authorities.

Over and over in the text, God encourages us to subject ourselves to our authority. *Subject* isn't a word we use often anymore (since we are no longer subjects of a king). Let's trade out that single word and see if the meaning of these verses becomes clearer.

Go back and read these verses again. Wherever you see the word *subject,* read it as *submit.*

Living in willing submission to our authorities doesn't come naturally. Ever since Eve ate the forbidden fruit and rebelled against God, our natural tendency is to resist authority and to rebel against rules and regulations. This is just one way God calls us to resist our sin-nature and live countercultural lives.

- We don't obey authority because we always feel like it.
- We don't obey our authorities because they are always right.
- We don't obey our authorities because they are perfect.

According to Romans 13:1, what is the primary reason we obey our authorities?

Think back to Deborah's story.

Who did God place in charge of the rebellion against Jabin (Judg. 4:6)?

Barak was a weak and fearful leader, yet Deborah followed his lead. Her encouraging words revealed her trust in God. So did her actions. She was free to submit because she knew God was her ultimate authority.

Unless your authorities clearly require you to violate God's law, God calls us to submit. What's the big deal about authority? Deborah points us toward an important truth: Our willingness to submit to human authority is an indicator of our willingness to submit to God's authority.

Pray through this list of authorities. Ask the Lord to help you trust Him more and to demonstrate that trust by gladly submitting to the people He has placed in charge of you.

- My parents
- My pastor
- My teachers
- My boss
- My government leaders

Write Romans 13:1 on an index card and place it somewhere you will see it often this week.

 *The Bigger Story*

God's Word is full of promises. Here are a few of my favorites.

- He will never leave or abandon us (Heb. 13:5).
- If we confess our sin, He will forgive us (1 John 1:9).
- He will come back for us (John 14:3).

What are some of your favorite promises from God's Word?

It's the nature of promises that we have to wait for them to come to pass. Many of the gifts God has for His people aren't yet ours for the taking.

A BEAUTIFUL DOWN PAYMENT

When you were little, did you ever make a promise and then say, "cross my heart, hope to die, stick a needle in my eye?" Sometimes kids say the strangest things! We're collectively skeptical in the promise department. We want proof that the promise will be delivered. Often, we take this approach with the promises of God. He has promised to meet our needs, to love us forever, to forgive our sins, and to prepare a place for us in heaven, yet we often long for a down payment of some sort that proves God will keep His word.

Deborah stepped out in faith and followed Barak into battle before she saw any evidence that the victory would be won in her favor. Deborah's enemy had 900 iron chariots and a large army of men prepared to fight (Judg. 4:13), but Deborah didn't trust her eyes. She didn't trust her feelings. She trusted the promises of God.

We can be more like Deborah in this way because Jesus has made a down payment. Check it out.

Rewrite 2 Corinthians 1:20-22 in your own words.

These verses give us two sources of "proof" that God will keep His promises. Highlight the phrase "every one of God's promises is 'Yes' in him."

Don't you just love that? Jesus Christ is the collateral for the promises of God. The cross stands as a reminder throughout all of time that He has done what He promised to do. He has given us His Holy Spirit as a guarantee of more to come, so that we could trust His promises fully. Our feelings or circumstances are not good indicators of God's willingness or ability to keep His promises. His sacrifice is. His Spirit is. We can be more like Deborah by choosing to trust the promises of God.

Look up each of the following promises. Write out the promise mentioned in each verse.

Psalm 50:5

Proverbs 18:10

Isaiah 26:3

Romans 8:28

Philippians 2:15

God Equips: A Beautiful Calling

Then David said to Abigail,
*"Blessed be the L*ORD *God of Israel,*
who sent you to meet me today!"
1 SAMUEL 25:32

STRETCH

I hope you're in your comfy pants, because for this session I'm inviting you into my living room. If you were really here, I'd pull a warm batch of cookies out of the oven just for you.

There's a big, cozy, green plaid chair in the corner—a sacred spot for me. I read my Bible in that seat most mornings. I get up early while my house is still quiet. (I have a husband, three children, two dogs, and two cats, so quiet is a hot commodity at my house!) I grab my Bible and a pen, a cup of hot tea, and dig in.

The method of study I use most often is called *annotating*. That's just a fancy way of saying *to add notes to*. I have a journaling Bible with wide, lined margins so I make my notes right in my Bible. You can make notes in a journal too, but I like to keep it all in one spot. Here's my specific method.

- I choose a book of the Bible and stick with it. I don't skip around. I read the entire book, little by little, making notes as I go.

- I look for repeated words or phrases. I underline or circle them.

- I also write out prayers in my Bible as I read.

- I once read about an elderly woman who wrote the letters T & P in her Bible every time she came to a promise that she knew to be "tried and proved." I love that idea! When I come across a promise I've seen God deliver on, I write a little T & P in my Bible. I have several Ts and Ps in my Bible!

I like this method because it forces me to slow down and soak up what I'm reading. I don't just want to cross reading my Bible off my to do list. I don't want to stand up from my green plaid chair and forget what I just read. This is God's Word! I want it to sink deeply into my heart and change the way I live. You too?

Of course, annotating isn't the only way to study God's Word. It's just the way I use most often. You'll get a chance to practice it in this session.

How do you like to study God's Word?

STORY I.D.

Read 1 Samuel 25. Fill in the details for Abigail in the following chart.

Who	Abigail
What	
When	
Where	
Why	

DIGGING DEEPER

After traveling for weeks, I was finally on my way home. All I could think about was seeing my family and sleeping in my own bed again. Then a storm hit, causing my flight to be canceled. I fought hot tears as I stood in line waiting for new flight information. I kept my cool until I stepped up to the counter and met the rude woman working the desk. Her attitude stunk! After a few minutes of her cranky behavior, my calm disguise cracked. I pointed my finger and said (loudly), "You don't have the right to be rude to me!" Then, I turned and marched myself in the opposite direction. As soon as I rounded the corner, I collapsed in a heap of tears. What is it about uncalled-for rudeness that rattles us so much?

Write about a time when you encountered uncalled-for rudeness. How did you respond?

As I look back on that airport encounter, I'm not proud of my response. If I had that moment to do over again, I would choose to respond with humility and kindness instead of anger and frustration. I wish I'd been more like Abigail.

Before we look at the details of Abigail's life, lets examine the backstory. David was anointed by the prophet Samuel as the next king of Israel (1 Sam. 16:1-13). That was good news for David, but it wasn't such good news for Saul, the reigning king of Israel. Knowing David would someday take his throne sent Saul into a jealous rage, and he set out to kill David (1 Sam. 23:15). David had an opportunity to kill Saul instead, but he didn't take it. He chose to honor Saul as his authority (1 Sam. 24:1-15).

David and his men were on the run and living in the wilderness when they met Abigail and her husband, Nabal.

Read 1 Samuel 25:3. Compare and contrast the character of Nabal with the character of Abigail.

Nabal's Character	Abigail's Character

Read 1 Samuel 25:4-8. What two words would you choose to describe the tone David instructed his men to use in their interaction with Nabal?

Read 1 Samuel 25:10-11. What two words would you choose to describe the tone Nabal used in his response to David's men?

Fast-forward a few verses to 1 Samuel 25:23-24. What two words would you choose to describe the tone Abigail used in her interaction with David?

I'd describe Abigail as humble and kind. God's Word encourages us to have the same attitude as Abigail. Humility can be a slightly tricky concept to grasp (and to live). It means to trade in our wants and needs for the wants and needs of others. We'll look more closely at humility in Session 7.

For a preview, let's read Colossians 3:12. What five virtues does this verse encourage us to "put on" as God's chosen ones?

List the specific ways Abigail demonstrated humility toward David.

TAKING THE HIPPOCRATIC OATH

Abigail didn't just respond to David with kindness and humility. She responded to her husband the same way, though it may not seem like it at first glance. Look back at Nabal's words to David's men in 1 Samuel 25:10-11.

Did Nabal make any specific commands?

He didn't. Nabal disrespected David's men—verse 14 even tells us "he screamed at them." Nabal didn't forbid Abigail from extending kindness to David. She honored her husband by intervening on his behalf when his actions were sure to bring trouble.

When her husband's actions threatened his home, his family, his fortune, and his safety, Abigail stepped up with kindness and humility to diffuse the situation. After David retreated and Abigail knew her husband was in the right frame of mind to receive the news, she told him what she had done rather than hiding it from him. The Bible says "his heart died" (1 Sam. 25:37). There are many reasons why Abigail's news might have affected Nabal so dramatically, but one possibility is that he realized his error and how close he came to grave danger as a result. Though Nabal was a harsh and badly behaved man, Abigail sought to do him good, not harm.

You don't have to be a wife for Proverbs 31:12 to apply to you. Maybe you've heard of the Hippocratic Oath. It's a vow doctors take committing to "do no harm" to their patients. We can adopt this same posture with our attitudes and words.

Rewrite Nabal's words to David from 1 Samuel 25:10-11 as if Nabal had committed to do no harm to others. Consider what he would have said differently.

LIVE LIKE DAUGHTERS OF THE KING

The primary difference between Nabal and Abigail wasn't in their words and attitudes, but in their hearts.

Read Luke 6:45 aloud.

Our words and actions reveal the true condition of our hearts. Let me show you what I mean. Grab your favorite pens—this is your chance to practice annotating!

Go back through 1 Samuel 25 and underline every time you see the word *lord* in lowercase. Circle every time you see the word *Lord* in uppercase.

Abigail referred to David as lord, showing him honor as the future king. But she referred to God as Lord, demonstrating her trust and surrender to Him.

If Abigail's words revealed what was on her heart, she was a woman fully surrendered to God as her true King and David as her future king. Eventually, Abigail became royalty herself, marrying David and accompanying him to the palace where he reigned for 40 years. But first, Abigail was a daughter of the true King. She was able to respond to a rude husband and to an angry future king with kindness and humility because she trusted the Lord.

TALK ABOUT IT

We cannot face difficult people gracefully on our own. Pride seems to come more naturally to us than humility. There are moments when each of us wants to respond with anger or bitterness rather than kindness. Abigail's story reminds us that it is only because of our relationship with the Lord that we can respond rightly to others.

Read John 14:26. Underline the role of the Holy Spirit. Circle the word Jesus used to describe the Holy Spirit.

Discuss the following questions with your group.

Describe someone you know who demonstrates exceptional kindness. What does her attitude reveal about her heart?

Describe someone you know who demonstrates exceptional humility. What does her attitude reveal about her heart?

Has there been a time when the Holy Spirit helped you to respond to someone with humility and kindness? Explain.

THINK ABOUT IT

Yes, God calls us to respond to others in ways that are countercultural and against the grain of our natural reactions, but He has given us a Helper to remind us of God's truth and equip us to live it out.

Take some time to ask the Holy Spirit to teach you how to respond with humility and kindness, especially toward those who do not deserve it.

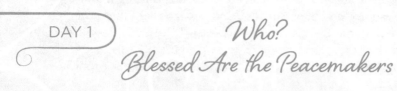

Who?
Blessed Are the Peacemakers

Read Matthew 5:1-11.

These verses are often called the "Beatitudes." Each one calls us to a specific response or attitude and promises a specific blessing in return. Mourning, humility, mercy—these may seem less desirable than a positive, can-do attitude, yet Jesus promises to reward these responses.

> Go back through the list of beatitudes. Highlight any attitude you see lived out in Abigail's life.

The quality I see most clearly in Abigail's life was *peacemaker*. Through her humble interaction with David, she went out of her way to create peace both in her home and in her land. Peace is mentioned countless times throughout the Bible. And Jesus is even described as the "Prince of Peace" (Isa. 9:6). Clearly, peace matters to God.

> Match the following verses with the correct reference.

John 14:27

If possible, as far as it depends on you, live at peace with everyone.

1 Corinthians 14:33

And the fruit of righteousness is sown in peace by those who cultivate peace.

Romans 12:18

God is not a God of disorder but of peace.

James 3:18

"Peace I leave with you. My peace I give to you."

What kind of peace does God value exactly? Is He talking about world powers or political policy when He references peace? Is He asking us to join the kind of peace movement that motivates people to march or rally?

The peace God calls us to is personal peace. The assurance that God is in control and He will keep His promises sets our hearts and minds at ease. As an outflow of our peace in Christ, God asks us to strive to live in harmony with others. Like Abigail, we are to place the needs of others above our own, to forgive freely and often, and to work toward reconciliation when conflict splinters our relationships.

ARE YOU A PEACEMAKER?

Answer the following questions to determine whether or not you are a peacemaker.

Does it seem like you are always in a fight with at least one of your friends?

Do you feel the need to verbalize it when someone upsets you, even if it is over something small?

Do you frequently find yourself in the middle of fights between your friends?

Do you need to apologize often for losing your temper or speaking unkindly?

Have you had several friendships end completely?

Do your social media posts create peace or conflict online?

If you answered "yes" to most of these questions, you probably have some work to do on the peacemaker front. We all do! Here are four rapid-fire ideas for how to be a peacemaker more often. Write out the verse for each one.

1. Let go of offenses (Prov. 19:11).

2. Say "I'm sorry" often (Jas. 5:16).

3. Forgive easily (Eph. 4:32).

4. Pray for those who cause conflict in your life (Matt. 5:44).

5. Do everything in your power to live at peace (Rom. 12:18).

DAY 2 — When? When Someone You Love is Caught in Sin

Do you have a "Nabal" in your life? Can you think of a family member or friend who is rebelling against the things of God and hurting themselves more in the process? We may not have the option to offer bread and sheep as a peace offering when someone we love is stuck in sin, so what can we do? Even when we don't have any other course of action available to us, we can pray.

What advice does Matthew 5:44 give to us?

Jot down the names of people you know and love who are stuck in sin. Commit to pray for them for the next ten days.

FIVE WAYS TO PRAY

Here are five ways, straight from Scripture, to pray for those stuck in sin. Write out each verse in your own words.

1. Pray for them to see their sin as God sees it: Isaiah 59:2

2. Pray for their hard hearts to soften: Ezekiel 36:26

3. Pray for them to recognize the kindness of God: Romans 2:4

4. Pray for them to have a desire for God's Word: Matthew 4:4

5. Pray for God's Word to do surgery in their hearts: Hebrews 4:12

TWO PRAYERS NOT TO PRAY

While you're praying, here are two prayers not to pray:

1. Get-'em-God prayers.

My pastor calls those prayers rooted in a desire for God to punish others "get-'em-God prayers." If someone you love has sinned against you, these kinds of prayers may be tempting.

Based on the character of Abigail, do you think she prayed for harm to come to Nabal? Why or why not?

Humility isn't a personality trait like being bubbly or funny. It is the response to understanding how big God is and how worthy He is of our worship. Because Abigail was fully surrendered to God, I suspect her prayers for her husband were wrapped in humility, not a desire to see Nabal harmed.

When we pray, let's keep in mind that God has forgiven us of much, even though we don't deserve it. That heart check will lead to humility, giving us the ability to pray for Him to forgive others, even if they've hurt us.

2. Splinter-eye prayers.

Read Matthew 7:3-5. Draw a picture of what this verse is describing.

Yes, Nabal was "harsh and evil in his dealings" (1 Sam. 25:3), while Abigail was "intelligent and beautiful" (1 Sam. 25:3), and David was the valiant future king, but one cord that connected them was that they were all sinners, just like us. (To get a glimpse of David's sin and a preview of Session 6, check out 2 Samuel 11.)

This is an important perspective when we are praying about the sin in someone else's life. If someone you know is stuck in sin, pray like crazy, but keep your own sin in mind.

Set aside time to pray for the people you listed earlier. Choose one Scripture from the list to pray for each individual.

When?
When You've "Screamed"

I have three little boys. With all that testosterone, the sibling rivalry can get a little intense in my house. At my wits' end with the unkind way my boys kept talking to each other, I recently gave a creative punishment. Each boy had to sit at the table with a paper plate, a toothpick, and a travel-sized tube of toothpaste. First, I made them squeeze all the toothpaste onto their plates. They thought that was fun, but they might not have if they had known what was coming next! Once the toothpaste was out of the tube I explained to them that they had to get all of the toothpaste back into the tube using the toothpick. They could not get up from the table until all of the toothpaste was back in.

I knew it was an impossible assignment. That was the point! Maybe you've heard our words described as the toothpaste inside the tube. Once they are out, there's no shoving them back in. That's why God's Word warns us to use our words with extreme caution.

> Describe a time when you said something you shouldn't. What was the result?

We need God's help to use our words to honor Him and others, but what can we do when we blow it? When we've "screamed" like Nabal, how can we make things right?

Proverbs is full of wisdom that can help us tame our tongues and make things right when we mess up. Look up each of the following Proverbs and jot down the specific action step you find in each verse. Highlight the verses that give specific advice for what to do when you've done damage with your words.

> Proverbs 6:2-3

> Proverbs 10:8

Proverbs 15:1

Proverbs 16:32

Proverbs 17:14

We need to address mistakes when we make them and respond with kindness and humility. This is never easy! We always need God's help, but addressing our mistakes is so worth it. If you've hurt others with your words, you can't undo it, but you can attempt to make it right. Here are two important steps to take.

1. Confess your sin to God.

When we sin against other people, we ultimately sin against God since all people bear His image. Don't wait until you are face to face with Him to give account for misusing your words. Tell Him right away.

According to 1 John 1:9, how does God promise to respond?

2. Ask for forgiveness.

When you've used your words harshly against someone else, own up to it. Take a page from Abigail's story and respond with kindness and humility.

What does James 5:16 encourage us to do?

THE EPHESIANS 4:29 PLEDGE

Read Ephesians 4:29. Ask the Lord to help you live this out starting now. Sign the Ephesians 4:29 pledge and ask the other members of your group to hold you accountable and champion you.

With God's help, I will strive to let no corrupting talk come out of my mouth. I will seek to only say words that build others up, fit the occasion, and give grace to those who hear.

_____ (Signed) _____ (Date)

DAY 4   *The Bigger Story*

Let's revisit Abigail's story for a moment. Specifically, let's look at how the story ended for Nabal.

> Reread 1 Samuel 25:36-38. What happened to Nabal?

> Reread 1 Samuel 25:39-42. What happened to Nabal's wife and by default his home, sheep, fortune, and so on?

Nabal refused to give David's men food and drink and ultimately he ended up losing so much more. This is how we like stories end. We want the "bad" guy to suffer and the "good" guy to ride off into the sunset with the girl.

> Write about your all-time favorite movie ending. What happened to the villain?

If Abigail's story were written as a Hollywood script, moviegoers would be satisfied. Yet this is not the end of Abigail's story. It's not the end of your story either.

> Read Romans 3:23. Highlight who has sinned.

Yes, Nabal was a sinner. So were David and Abigail. They all needed God's grace equally. It's tempting to villainize Nabal and celebrate Abigail, but the gospel helps us remember three key truths.

1. Nabal and Abigail were both made in the image of God (Gen. 1:27).

2. God loved Nabal and Abigail (Isa. 43:4-5).

3. God wants everyone to be saved (1 Tim. 2:3-4).

An important tenant of understanding the gospel is found in Romans 3:10.

> *There is no one righteous, not even one.*

Swap out the word *righteous* (which simply means to do right) with good and read that passage again. According to God's Word, there are no good guys (or girls). That doesn't make much sense when we compare our "goodness" with the people around us, but when we compare our good deeds, good behaviors, and good words with Jesus', we suddenly see they aren't good at all.

> *All of us have become like one who is unclean, and all*
> *our righteous acts are like filthy rags; we all shrivel up*
> *like a leaf, and like the wind our sins sweep us away.*
> ISAIAH 64:6, NIV

What does Isaiah 64:6 compare our good deeds to?

It's like when you think an old t-shirt is white until you hold it up next to a new, bright white shirt. Suddenly, your white t-shirt looks like a dingy rag. This is how our goodness looks compared to the righteousness of Christ.

It's easy to point fingers and see how Nabal's words got him into trouble. But let's point that finger back at ourselves for a moment.

Write out the sobering truth found in Matthew 12:36.

We will have to fess up to every idol word. Can you imagine?

Because of the gospel, our careless words won't keep us out of heaven. We are accepted because of Jesus, but Scripture indicates that we will see the toothpaste out of the tube. We will realize the impact our words had for good or for bad.

One lesson Abigail's story teaches is our universal need for grace. We all fall short and miss the mark God has for us. We all need Him to intervene or we will flush our own lives straight down the toilet. Nabal may be the villain, but his story is a reminder of how much we all need God's grace.

God Redeems: A Beautiful Mess

*God, create a clean heart for me
and renew a steadfast spirit within me.*
PSALM 51:10

STRETCH

Match the following main characters with the correct book or movie.

Woody	Star Wars
Dorothy	To Kill a Mockingbird
Luke Skywalker	Toy Story
Belle	The Chronicles of Narnia
Atticus Finch	The Wizard of Oz
Aslan	Beauty and the Beast

When we study God's Word, it is tempting to see the individuals as the main characters. We might see Noah as the main character in the story of the Ark or Jonah as the main character in the story of the whale. We often read God's Word, asking questions in this order:

1. Who is this story about?

2. What does this passage teach me about myself?

3. What can we learn about God from this story?

To truly understand the Bible, we need to invert the pyramid, shifting what we feel is most important to the bottom and elevating God to the most important slot. When we make this shift, we see that God is the main character of the Bible. Every story is designed to teach us something about Him.

Fill in the blanks for 1 Corinthians 8:6.

"Yet for us there is _____ God, the _____. _____ things are _____ him, and _____ exist _____ him. And there is _____ Lord, _____ _____. _____ things are through _____, and _____ exist _____ him."

According to this passage, all of mankind was created from God and for God. Our stories were written to point to Him. With that big idea in mind, I train myself to ask new questions, in a new order, as I study God's Word. These three questions apply to every passage in the Bible and help us to look for the higher story. Let's intentionally ask these questions as we dig into Bathsheba's story together in this session.

1. What does this tell me about God?

2. What does this tell me about us (the church)?

3. What should our response be?

Don't flip the order, looking for clues about *yourself* and *your* purpose first. The Bible is not primarily a story about us; it is primarily a story about Jesus. When we see Him as the main character and ourselves in a supporting role, we are able to handle God's Word "correctly."

STORY I. D.

Read 2 Samuel 11–12. Fill in the details for Bathsheba in the chart.

Who	Bathsheba
What	
When	
Where	
Why	

DIGGING DEEPER

Shylah got pregnant the summer after she graduated high school. While her classmates joined club sports teams and met up with new friends at the coffee shop, Shylah hid in her dorm room and wrestled with how to tell her parents about the baby. Shylah made a mistake. She missed God's mark for purity and she would pay a heavy price.

She married her high school boyfriend and delivered a beautiful blonde baby boy, but Shylah's happy ending arrived slowly, not suddenly. Her marriage didn't last and Shylah carried around the heavy burdens of shame and rejection for a long time.

Shylah is one of my very best friends. She is beautiful and fun. She's a great mom and a great friend. She has laid those heavy burdens down and exchanged them for something better. Hers is not a story of shame, but of redemption. That is only possible because she is not the main character of her story, God is.

EMBRACE THE MESS

Perhaps your story doesn't involve an unplanned pregnancy like Shylah's or an affair with the king like Bathsheba's, but every story has its messy side. In addition to digging deep into Bathsheba's story, we're going to peel back the layers of Psalm 51, a song written by David after his affair with Bathsheba was exposed.

David didn't sugarcoat his situation or gloss over his sin. He acknowledged the mess he was in.

> Read Psalm 51:3-5. Discuss the ways David talked about sin in this passage and what this means for the ways we should talk about sin in our own lives.

Our messy state isn't fun to think about, but looking away doesn't change the fact that our hearts and lives are messy. Bathsheba's story shows us that our messes can be beautiful, because they pave a way for God's glorious redemption.

Bathsheba's story does have the happiest of endings, but it may take us awhile to see it. With a sexual affair between a king and another man's wife, a murder, and the death of a baby, this is not an easy story to read or discuss. It's messy! But let's remind ourselves of the truth we uncovered in Session 3.

Read 2 Timothy 3:16 aloud.

What portion of Scripture is God-breathed and useful? Some of it? Most of it? Nope. All Scripture is God-breathed and useful for our instruction. That means we choose not to skip over the parts that make us squirm. Instead, we read closely, looking for clues about the character of God even when the plotline is messy. Let's start digging!

SHE'S OUT OF CONTROL

Like many of the women we've looked at in this study, Bathsheba did not have control over many of the details of her own life. Look back over her Story I.D. chart.

> Circle anything about Bathsheba's profile that she could not control.

Bathsheba could not control that King David summoned her. What do you think would have happened to Bathsheba if she had refused to come to the palace?

She likely did not have control over what happened next either. As the king, David could take whatever or whomever he wanted in the kingdom. She did not have control over whether she became pregnant or over David's response to the news that she was carrying his baby. She could not control David's decision to have her husband killed. Once she and David were married and their child became sick, she could not control whether or not he would get well.

> What parts of your life make you feel out of control? Write about them here and discuss them with your group.

In this moment, your life may not feel quite as out of control as Bathsheba's must have, but none of us have as much control as we like to think.

> Read Isaiah 45:6-7. Who is ultimately in charge of all things?

David and Bathsheba's affair, Uriah's murder, and the death of David and Bathsheba's baby—these things were not God's plan. Skim back through Bathsheba's story.

> List any verses that indicate this mess was outside of God's will for David and Bathsheba.

Even though David chose to step outside of God's best for Him, God remained in control. We cannot dethrone God with our bad decisions. This gives us great hope!

If we were friends with Bathsheba at the moment her baby boy died, I imagine we'd be very worried about her. Her story seemed hopeless at that moment. If we went to the palace to comfort her she might whisper, "How could God redeem this mess?"

What would you say to her in that moment?

UNDERSTANDING REDEMPTION

Grab a dictionary to look up the word *redeem*. Record what you find.

My favorite definition for redeem is "to buy back: repurchase."[1] We'll explore the wonder of this definition in your devotions this week, but for now lets think of redemption as to repair or restore, to set right.

Read Psalm 130:7. Highlight the word that describes God's redemption. Underline the word that describes His love.

God is a redeeming God. He loves to set things right. He is motivated by steadfast love toward those who bear His image. Because of this, He extends plentiful redemption toward us.

Let's dig a little deeper. Grab a thesaurus or find an online version and jot down synonyms for the word *plentiful*.

God isn't stingy with redemption. He extends it to us in abundance! But He doesn't always offer quick redemption. The process often takes a while. The difficult circumstances Bathsheba faced could not be undone, but God did not leave her as a grieving wife and mother forever. Let's fill in the details of the rest of Bathsheba's story.

Read the following passages and record the blessings
Bathsheba received.

2 Samuel 12:24-25

1 Kings 1:28-31

Bathsheba went on to become Solomon's mom. Her husband, David, reigned
as king for forty years and at her request, her son took over the throne even
though David had an older son named Adonijah.

God redeemed Bathsheba's losses. That's the lower story. How do
you see Bathsheba's story pointing to the gospel? What parallels
can you draw between Bathsheba's redemption and your own?

TALK ABOUT IT

Tell a story about a time when God redeemed your broken
heart or a broken relationship.

What do we learn about God when we don't skip over the
messy sections of the Bible?

What messes are you facing in your own life right now where
you need help trusting God for redemption? How can we pray
for you in this mess?

THINK ABOUT IT

God would continue to bring restoration and redemption to the house of
David long after Bathsheba was gone. We'll dig into this later this week,
but for now consider how the mess of Bathsheba's life allowed God
to intervene.

Read Romans 8:28. What parts of your life does God promise
to work out for your good?

Revisit the list of things that make you feel out of control. Ask
God to show you how He is redeeming these areas for your
good. Share your answers with the group.

Who?
Unlikely Experts on Redemption

Remember my friend, Shylah? I shared her story about getting pregnant as a teenager at the beginning of this session. Shylah is passionate about ministering to young women with messy lives. When I asked her if I could include her story in this study she said, "Yes, yes, yes! I'm so honored that God could maybe use this to help someone else. He is such a good God!"

I told you that Shylah has traded in her burdens of shame and rejection for something better. Actually, God is the one who initiated that exchange. Remember that one definition for redemption is to "buy back." Because of His sacrifice on the cross, Jesus paid the price so my friend didn't need to carry these burdens any longer. As she has studied His Word, she's embraced that redemption: trading in shame for approval and rejection for acceptance. She boldly tells her story because she knows the details of her life are just the lower story. They point to the higher story of Christ's redemptive work.

Take some time to read all of Psalm 51. Remember that David penned these words right after his sin was exposed. To help you focus, annotate the passage making note of anything that sticks out to you.

Now, invert the pyramid. Don't look at this like a song about a man who sinned, but as a song about a God who redeems. With that POV in mind, answer the following:

What does this tell me about God?

What does this tell me about us (the church)?

What should our response be?

Focus on verses 13-14.

Then I will teach the rebellious your ways,
and sinners will return to you.
Save me from the guilt of bloodshed, God—
God of my salvation—
and my tongue will sing of your righteousness.

What did David promise to do if God would redeem him?

He promised to tell! Next to these verses in my Bible I've written, "my mess will be my message." Our messy lives work like a microphone held up to God's redemption. The messier our story gets, the greater the opportunity for God to showcase His plan for redemption.

Because we are sinners in great need of salvation, we are the right people to tell of the redemption of God. We've experienced it firsthand. We are no longer just investigating the story; we are eyewitnesses to His goodness and grace.

I love Psalm 107:2. It's one of the main reasons why I write Bible studies like this one. Read this verse and write it out in your own words.

Let the redeemed of the Lord tell their story—those he redeemed from the hand of the foe. PSALM 107:2, NIV

Like David, we are free to declare that if God will redeem us (and He will) we will share the story. Our mess is our message because Christ does not leave us in our mess.

Imagine you are Bathsheba. Record her story, focusing on all the ways God has redeemed her mess.

Now that you've had some practice, write out your own story in a paragraph or two. How has God redeemed your mess?

DAY 2 — What? Even This?

Aly is a Christian. She's a straight A student. She has always been involved in her church. Two years ago, Aly was living a double life. She was dating a non-Christian behind her parents' backs. The relationship turned physical. This led her to make other compromises including drinking alcohol. She hid her sin for months, but eventually the truth came out.

Aly had to endure a painful process of repentance and making things right. But as she did, God did something amazing! He gave her opportunities to share her struggles with other teenagers who needed to hear that they could experience forgiveness for their secret sins. When I asked Aly if I could write about her story she said, "If one girl chooses God's truth because of my story, it would all be worth it to me." God took Aly's mess and turned it into a message about His forgiveness.

It shouldn't surprise us when God works this way. He promises in His Word that He will. Let's revisit Romans 8:28. Fill in the blanks below.

> We _____ that all things work _____ for the good of those who _____ God, who are _____ according to _____ purpose.

This verse is loaded with God's promises. Let's dig them out.

Who are God's promises made to in this verse?

What did God specifically promise?

When will God's promises come true?

Where will we be when we realize God's promises?

Why does God promise these things to us?

If you struggled with the last three questions, that's okay. The answers weren't in the text. Where and when God will redeem our mess, often remains a mystery, but we can count on Him to do it, because He loves us and because He always keeps His word.

Maybe like Aly or Shylah there is sin in your life that you look at and think, "How can God use this for my good?" The promise of Scripture is that God has a plan for you, and there's nothing in your life that He can't use.

YOUR REDEMPTION MISSION

Are there parts of your life that are messy? Are there areas of past sin? If so, explain.

Have you experienced pain, trials, or heartbreak? If so, explain.

What is something in your life right now that you question God's ability to redeem?

Write out 2 Corinthians 1:3-4.

God comforts us. We comfort others. It's a simple mission, but one you can accept right now. Do you want to do something big for God's kingdom today? Find someone who is going through something you've been through and find a way to comfort them. We all have messes. The question is, will we let God use them to share His message?

Who can you share your story of redemption with today? Write them a text or note.

When? Wait for the Lord

Picture your favorite meal. I see a big, juicy steak and a loaded baked potato. *Yum!* Your favorite meal might not be the same as mine, but I can almost guarantee it isn't made in a microwave. No one selects leftovers or TV dinners for their favorite meal. The good stuff always takes a while.

That's certainly the case with redemption. God rarely works out redemption in a microwave. Often it takes years, sometimes it takes generations. Let's look back over the lives of the women we've already studied. Redemption is a theme in every single story, though it rarely happens quickly.

Let's start with Eve.

> What was Eve's mess?

> How did God redeem it?

True redemption for Eve's sin took thousands of years. It wasn't until Jesus' death on the cross that the penalty was ultimately paid for that forbidden fruit.

Let's think about Hagar.

> What was Hagar's mess?

> How did God redeem it?

Remember that Hagar was sent back to live with her bitter owner only to deliver a baby who would never be accepted. In many ways, we are still waiting for the redemption of Hagar's story as Ishmael and Isaac's descendants remain at odds with each other.

What about Miriam?

> What messes did Miriam find herself in?

> How did God redeem it?

Miriam did experience some quick redemption. She watched her enemies drown in the sea, but she had to wait for the promised land. Her people wandered in the desert for 40 years. Miriam died before her people saw the full redemption of their captivity.

Consider Abigail.

What was her mess?

How did God redeem it?

Abigail's partial redemption was quick compared to the other women we've looked at. Her ill-behaved husband was replaced with a righteous king. But that's the lower story. Remember that the higher story is Abigail's need for redemption from her sin. She would need this kind of redemption over and over again.

That brings us back to Bathsheba.

What was her mess?

How did God redeem it?

There are sections of Bathsheba's story that were redeemed over a period of months, some took years, but her complete redemption would take much longer. As we will see in tomorrow's devotion, Jesus, the Redeemer, would come from Bathsheba's family line. God used her to play a part in the redemption of all mankind, but His redemption did not come quickly. Twenty-eight generations lived and died between David and Jesus (Matt. 1:17). This might feel like painfully slow redemption to us, but Scripture urges us to rethink our understanding of slow.

Summarize 2 Peter 3:9 in your own words.

When you are waiting for God to set something right, the wait can feel unbearable, but these stories help us see that God will keep His promise to redeem. It may not be on our timetable, but He will work all things to our good; He will redeem our messes.

We have redemption through the blood of Christ right now. We don't have to wait for it any longer. But we may have to wait for Him to redeem the circumstances of our individual lives.

Psalm 27:14 is a beautiful prayer to pray for those who are waiting on the Lord. Meditate on its words as you illustrate the verse in your journal.

DAY 4 — *The Bigger Story*

You've been studying these women for several weeks now, so it's time to put your skills to the test. Dig through the details and find the higher story in Jesus' lineage. You're looking for Jesus, the gospel, and God's plan for redemption at work. To find it, you need to fill in a family tree.

Turn to Matthew 1:1-16. This passage traces the genealogy of Jesus, starting with Abraham. Then, beginning with Solomon (v. 6), list David and Bathsheba's descendants below.

Solomon, _____

_____

_____

_____, *Jacob*

Go back through the list and circle any women who are mentioned.

Who is Uriah's wife mentioned in verse 6? (*Hint: Review 2 Samuel 3:11*).

Fill in the blanks for Matthew 1:16.

And _____ fathered _____ the husband of _____,, who gave birth to _____ who is called _____ _____.

MESS TO MESSIAH

Jesus is a direct descendant of David and Bathsheba. Their names are forever carved into the roots of His family tree. Remember how David and Bathsheba's relationship started? It began with sexual sin that sent out shock waves including murder, deception, and deep grief. What a mess!

Revisit the curse handed down to David by the prophet Nathan in 2 Samuel 12:10-13. Write out the details.

In one breath Nathan announced David's punishment, but in the next he promised David and Bathsheba's redemption, vowing that God would take away their sin and spare their lives. This first act of mercy worked like a domino, setting others in motion until Jesus' arrival.

David's sin worked like a magnifying glass exposing his need for a Savior. We may never have an adulterous relationship or order the murder of a fellow image bearer, but we need a Savior too. We desperately need to be redeemed from our sin nature. We need Jesus!

Can you believe the Savior of the world was born from grandparents who met through an adulterous relationship? Are you shocked that the Messiah was born out of such a mess? What a beautiful picture of redemption! Jesus didn't come to polish up our already clean hearts. He came to rescue us from the mess of sin and to redeem us as His image bearers.

Remember how I told you that my favorite definition for redemption was to buy back? That's exactly what Christ did for each of us on the cross. He paid the debt created by our sin. He bought us back from sin and death through His tremendous sacrifice on the cross. He redeemed us!

YOUR REDEMPTION STORY

Read 1 Timothy 1:12-16. How did Paul describe himself in verse 13?

If you described yourself in terms of your sin what words would you use?

When we look closely at our sin, we might feel as hopeless as Bathsheba must have at the graveside of her baby boy. "How can God redeem this?" our hearts whisper. But He can! He has!

Write out 1 Timothy 1:15. Who did Jesus come into the world to save?

Sketch out your family tree. How do you see God's redemption in the story of your family?

God Opposes: A Beautiful Showdown

But he gives greater grace.
Therefore he says: God resists the
proud, but gives grace to the humble.
JAMES 4:6

STRETCH

List your top five favorite things. These can be people, books, possessions, hobbies, and so on—if you love it, list it.

1.

2.

3.

4.

5.

I'm guessing very few of your favorite things will make it to the million year mark. Most won't even be around in the next fifty or one hundred years. It's okay to love these things, but it's not wise to put our hope in things that are temporary. God's Word helps us to hold on to what will last.

THESE THINGS REMAIN

Our achievements will fade away. Our possessions will rot. Our relationships will change. That reality can make us feel like we are standing on the epicenter of an earthquake, but God's Word steadies our feet.

Look up each of the following verses. Jot down something temporary listed in each verse.

Matthew 24:35	2 Peter 3:10	Revelation 21:4

Look up each of the following verses. Record something permanent listed in each verse.

Exodus 15:18	Isaiah 40:8	1 Peter 1:25

Most of what we can see with our eyes is destined to pass away. The Bible calls everything in this category "former things." They will not last forever. Knowing so much of my life is temporary helps me to shift my focus toward the eternal. What will last forever?

1. God

2. The Word of God

3. The People of God

In this session, we will investigate Jezebel, a woman determined to put an end to God, His Word, and His people. Her story helps us to see that, although everything else eventually fades away, these three things will always remain. God is unchangeable. His Word is unbreakable. His people are unstoppable. These truths make us brave and help us to fight even the most determined enemies.

STORY I.D.

Fill out two Story I.D. charts. First, examine Ahab, a wicked king who ruled over Israel more than one hundred years after King David.[1] Find the details of Ahab's character in 1 Kings 16:29-31.

Who   Ahab

What

When

Where

Why

Ahab's wife was Jezebel. We'll follow their story through several chapters in 1 and 2 Kings, but first we'll fill in some general details from 1 Kings 16:29-31.

Who   Jezebel

What

When

Where

Why

DIGGING DEEPER

It's time for a quick physics lesson. Newton's Third Law states simply: "For every action in nature there is an equal and opposite reaction."[2]

Let's think of it a different way. Your body and your chair are acting out Newton's Third Law right now. Your body is pushing against your chair and your chair is pushing against your body. That allows you to sit and read these words. If the action of your body pushing into your chair was not equally met with the action of the chair pushing into your body, you'd fall on the floor.

When this delicate balance of equal and opposite force is upset, things go haywire. There's a spiritual principle embedded in this physical law.

Read James 4:6. What's the word used to describe God's action toward the proud?

He pushes back against the proud. Pride is the part of each one of us that wants to run the show, to be in charge and make the rules rather than surrendering to God's sovereignty and plans for our lives. Pride tempts us to push back against the Word of God and the rules He has established for our good.

As we will see in Jezebel's story, God doesn't respond to pride with an equal and opposite force, keeping things in balance. He responds like a fire hose against a dripping faucet.

Let's look at the backstory in 1 Kings 16:29-34.

> But Ahab son of Omri did what was evil in the LORD's sight more than all who were before him. 1 KINGS 16:30

Ahab was an exceedingly wicked king! But what was his sin exactly? This passage gives us two clues.

According to verse 31, in whose sins did Ahab walk?

Jeroboam was another king of Israel. His story can be found in 1 Kings 11–14. Specifically, 1 Kings 12:16-24 tells us that Jeroboam committed four specific sins. List Jeroboam's actions in each of the following passages.

1 Kings 12:28

1 Kings 12:31a

1 Kings 12:31b

1 Kings 12:33

These offenses might seem minor at first glance, but each of them was a violation of God's commands. God was angered when His people worshiped a golden calf during the time of Moses. Jeroboam doubled this offense. Temples, priests, feasts were to stick to God's strict guidelines, and yet Jeroboam made up his own rules for how God's people would worship. By the time Ahab took the throne, God's people were in full rebellion against the things of God and worshiped the false god, Baal.

> Read 1 Kings 16:32-33. What did Ahab have built to honor Baal?

As the leader of Israel, Ahab led God's people away from worshiping the true God and toward worshiping false gods. Jezebel was not an innocent bystander to her husband's wicked ways. When we dig deeply into her story, we see that she encouraged her husband's bad behavior.

Elijah was the prophet assigned to call out Ahab and Jezebel's sin. You might remember him from your devotions in Session 4 as the man who heard God speak in a still, small whisper. We'll learn more about him in your devotions, but for now let's look at how Jezebel treated Elijah and his message.

> Read 1 Kings 19:1-3. What did Jezebel threaten to do to Elijah?

Elijah is not the only man Jezebel wanted to see ruined.

> Read 1 Kings 21:1-16. What did Jezebel do to Naboth?

> What motivated her to take this action?

When Elijah opposed her false religion, Jezebel threatened murder. When Naboth failed to give her husband something he wanted, Jezebel arranged for Naboth to be stoned to death.

> Read 2 Kings 9:30. This was the beginning of the end for Jezebel. Jehu was the king who replaced her husband, Ahab. How did Jezebel treat Jehu?

When she wanted something from Jehu, she put on makeup, fixed her hair, and tried to use her beauty to her advantage. As an image bearer, she was uniquely designed to showcase beauty. She didn't use her beauty to draw attention to God, but rather to draw attention to herself.

Pride oozes out of every crevice of Jezebel's story. She rebelled against human authority. She manipulated others to get what she wanted. She worshiped false gods who did not call her to righteous living. Ultimately, these were all just symptoms of her rebellion against the one true God.

What does the Bible say about pride?

Isaiah 2:12

Proverbs 11:2

Proverbs 16:5

OPPOSES THE PROUD

Jezebel seemed to have everything going for her including beauty, success, power, and money. And yet, her plans failed. God opposed her. He worked against her. Though she had every resource at her fingertips, her plans were thwarted, but God's were not.

In 1 Kings 21:17-24, God spoke through Elijah to condemn Ahab and Jezebel's actions concerning Naboth's vineyard. On the left side of the following chart list the specific punishments Elijah prophesied for Ahab and Jezebel. We will revisit this chart in a moment and see that nothing can stop the plans of God.

Punishment Prophesied for Ahab	Punishment Realized for Ahab
• 1 Kings 21:19	• 1 Kings 22:34-38
• 1 Kings 21:21-22	• 2 Kings 9:24 (Joram was the final descendant of Ahab's line to reign as king.)
Punishments Prophesied of Jezebel	Punishment Realized for Jezebel
• 1 Kings 21:23-24	• 2 Kings 9:30-37

Despite their power, wealth, and fury, Ahab and Jezebel could not stop God's judgment. Go back and fill out the right side of the chart with the punishments Ahab and Jezebel received.

Jezebel seemed to have it all, yet her pride became like a boa constrictor around her life, squeezing out the blessings and purpose God had for her. Though God gifted her with a throne, a husband, beauty, and wealth, He took it all from her, allowing her to die a gruesome terrible death because her pride kept her from surrendering her will to His will. It did not matter how much force she applied toward God, she could not push back against His judgment.

What warning does Proverbs 16:18 give?

These words perfectly describe Jezebel's fate. Her pride paved the way for her destruction, literally leading to her fall from a tower to her death. What a gory and gut-wrenching picture of what happens when we allow pride to keep us from worshiping the God who made us.

TALK ABOUT IT

Discuss the following questions with your group.

How might Jezebel's story have ended differently if she had responded to the Lord with humility rather than pride?

In what ways do you see pride in your own life?

What is your reaction to the truth that God opposes or works against the proud?

THINK ABOUT IT

Take some time to journal a prayer to God asking Him to expose areas of pride in your life. Ask God to help you surrender to Him and His will for your life and avoid the destruction that pride always brings.

Who?
Who Can Stand Against Us?

If Jezebel was the evil villain in this story, Elijah was the superhero determined to defeat evil. Remember, Elijah was the prophet God asked to call Ahab and Jezebel back to a pure worship of God. He made many attempts to reach Ahab and Jezebel with the truth, but one attempt stands out as the true showstopper.

Check out 1 Kings 18:17-40. There's a lot going on in this passage, so don't rush through it. Take your time, pausing to ask yourself often: What does this tell me about God?

> According to verse 19, how many prophets of Baal met Elijah on Mount Carmel? How many prophets of Asherah met Elijah at Mount Carmel?

Quick math reveals that Elijah was up against 850 prophets. The odds of a victory weren't exactly stacked in his favor. Elijah didn't call for this showdown simply to put the other prophets in their place or to embarrass Ahab. He clearly explained his goal in verse 21. Elijah wanted to put God on display. This should be the goal of every image bearer. We were made by God to bring glory to God.

> What did the prophets of Baal do to try to get their god to respond (vv. 23-29)?

Despite their desperate attempts to bring glory to Baal, he did not respond. He couldn't! He was a figment of their imagination, an idol created to serve their own purposes.

> When it was Elijah's turn, he built an altar and soaked it with so much water that the altar overflowed. Why do you think Elijah took this step?

Elijah wanted to prove beyond a shadow of a doubt that the God he worshiped is the one true God.

Write out Elijah's prayer from verses 36-37 in your own words.

How did God respond (v. 38)?

How did the people respond (v. 39)?

God was glorified! The people were amazed by God's power and worshiped Him on the mountain where Baal's prophets had just been defeated. The prophets of Baal tried everything to tip the outcome in their favor, but the plans of God and the people of God cannot be stopped.

From cover to cover, the Bible is full of stories of people who loved God and were opposed by man. Yet no man or woman in history, no matter how powerful, can snatch God's people out of His hand or stop Him from fulfilling His promises to us. This reality is what inspired the psalmist to write:

> In God I trust; I will not be afraid. What can mere humans do to me? PSALM 56:11

Elijah was not the first to be persecuted for his faith in God. He won't be the last. You will likely face times when your faith is questioned, mocked, or discouraged. You may never face 850 angry prophets, but you may have moments when living your life for God's glory is not easy. The only way you will have the courage to stand up to those who oppose you is to trust that your God will come through. Man's attacks are temporary. Let's remind ourselves what is permanent.

Flip back to the beginning of this session. List the three things that will last forever.

Think through the following areas of your life. How can you bring God glory in each area?

Your social media platforms:

Your talents and goals for the future:

Your interactions with family and friends:

DAY 2) *What? The Antidote to Pride*

I hope Jezebel's story inspires you to deal with pride in your own life. None of us wants to share her fate. But how can you know if you have a pride problem? I've developed a not-so-scientific method to check.

Take two fingers and place them just below your jaw line. Do you feel that *thump, thump, thump, thump*? That's your pulse. If you have a pulse, you have a pride problem. We all do! A by-product of our sin nature is to want to focus on ourselves rather than on the One who created us.

Pride can be like a poison, spreading through our lives and killing God's best for us, but there is an antidote. You've already learned a lot about it—it's humility. Remember how Abigail demonstrated humility? Take a moment to review your notes on humility from Session 5.

We can't just decide to be humble. The poison has spread too far for that. We have to pry our eyeballs away from ourselves and toward something greater.

Let's look at Revelation 4:1-11. This is one of my favorite passages, because it immediately puts our pride into check.

Read the entire passage. Go slowly. Take your time. Highlight anything that jumps out at you.

How is God described in this passage?

How about you? Where are you in the throne room? Where is your crown and throne?

You're not even there. The reality of the power and wonder of God should cause us to respond in humility.

1. We are not on the throne, but God is.

2. We are limited, but God is limitless.

3. We are small, but God is huge!

4. We are sinners, but God is holy, holy, holy.

Read Philippians 2:3-8. Record the practical advice given for how to live with humility.

Humility recognizes that the universe exists for Jesus, not for us. In response to that truth, instead of living me-centrically, we follow His example and put others first.

Specifically, what action steps does this passage encourage us to take?

Do you need a dose of humility? Is pride making you sick? Let me give you a few prompts to help you think that through.

- The way I spend my free time.
- The way I talk to my parents.
- The way I talk to my siblings.
- The way I spend my money.
- What I think about most often.
- Who I am online.
- My goals for my friendships.

For each one of these areas are you:

- Sick with pride (me-centric thinking)? If so, write a P beside it.
- Vaccinated with humility (putting others first)? If so, write an H beside this prompt.
- Somewhere in the middle? Draw a star.

If you drew a star or a P in an area, that's somewhere you need God to vaccinate you against pride. Take a minute and ask for His help in this area right now. Journal a prayer and come back to it every day this week.

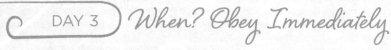
DAY 3 — *When? Obey Immediately*

Remember that Jesus is the main character of every story—your story, my story, and even Jezebel's story. In her case, we may see that truth more clearly if we shift our point of view. Let's look again at the life of Elijah. God's story is written all over it!

Imagine we have a scrapbook of Elijah's life. Let's mentally flip through a few pages and look at some snapshots.

Read 1 Kings 17:3-6.

What did God command Elijah to do?

How did Elijah respond?

Pick up the story in 1 Kings 17:7-16.

What did God command Elijah to do?

How did Elijah respond?

Read 1 Kings 17:17-24.

What did Elijah ask God to do?

How did God respond?

Read 1 Kings 19:2-8.

What did God's messengers ask Elijah to do?

How did he respond?

Read 1 Kings 19:16-19.

Who did God command Elijah to train as his successor?

What did Elijah do?

Imagine walking a mile in his sandals for a moment. How might you respond if God asked you to do as he commanded Elijah? I might drag my feet, pretend I didn't hear the Lord correctly, obey partially, or even rebel completely. Yet, every time, no matter how strange God's command was or what dangers it put Elijah in, he responded with immediate obedience.

Imagine what could have happened if he delayed. If he had waited to go to the brook, he would have been caught in a drought. If he had waited to visit the widow, she and her son would have starved to death. Elijah's story helps us to see the benefits of immediately obeying the Lord.

A CALL TO OBEY

Immediate obedience is what God asks of us. He wants us to live our lives like Elijah, obeying immediately every time, even when we cannot see God's plan clearly.

Check out the dramatic ending to Elijah's story found in 2 Kings 2:1-12.

Obedience paved the way for Elijah to live the grand adventure God planned for him. He saw miracle after miracle. He spent months of drought beside his very own bubbling brook. He received food from ravens and angels. He witnessed a dead boy raised back to life. He single-handedly took down the prophets of Baal. He saw a wicked and oppressive government removed from power. He parted the river with his cloak. He entered heaven on a chariot of fire, pulled by horses of fire. Amazing! None of this would have been possible without his immediate obedience. Every time he obeyed, God used Elijah to do big things. As a result, his story pointed to the much higher story of God at work.

Psalm 119:68 reminds us that God is good. It is a prayer to learn God's Word so that we can obey Him more fully. Write out this verse as a prayer to wrap up today's study.

DAY 4   *The Bigger Story*

The gospel is the thread that binds the whole Bible together. It might be difficult to see it in a story about a pagan ruler who lived almost a thousand years before Jesus was born. Let's insert ourselves into Jezebel's story and see what we find.

Revisit 1 Kings 16:31-33.

Jezebel was a Sedonian. Her people group no longer exists, but the Bible gives us some clues about who they were.

- They lived in the promised land when God's people arrived under the command of Joshua (Josh. 13:4-6).
- God left them in the land to test Israel's obedience. The Israelites failed the test and instead of driving out the Sedonians, they adopted many of their religious rituals toward other gods (Judg. 3:3-6).
- They were timber cutters who had a reputation for excellent work (1 Kings 5:6; 1 Chron. 22:4; Ezra 3:7).

Let me describe Jezebel's people in modern language.

- They lived and worked alongside God's people, though they did not share the same beliefs or values.
- They worshiped things other than the one true God. Examples might include money, power, popularity, and outer beauty.
- They prided themselves on productivity.

    What about Jezebel herself? Can we draw any parallels between her and ourselves?

Jezebel worshiped the false god of Baal by bowing at an altar and Asherah pole. This violates one of the Ten Commandments.

    Write out Exodus 20:3.

    What does Leviticus 26:1 command?

We may not bow to stone statues or worship beneath a pole, but are we really that different from Jezebel? Anything or anyone we think we cannot live without is an object of our worship.

Pause and ask the Lord to reveal any idols in your life. List them here.

Jezebel was more than an idol worshiper. She was a murderer. Remember that she arranged to have Naboth stoned to death in order to take his vineyard and threatened to kill Elijah (1 Kings 19:1-2; 21:8-14). It's easy to think we are better than Jezebel since we've never plotted another person's murder, but Jesus asks us to dig deeper and see the wickedness that lies in the depths of our hearts.

Look up Matthew 5:21-26. What sins did Jesus list as offenses in addition to murder?

Read 1 John 3:15. What does this verse call those who hate their brothers?

You may never plot the murder of a neighbor, but is there someone you hate? Is there anyone you are bitter toward? Is there someone you've insulted? God's Word calls you a murderer.

Remember Jezebel's beauty? Let's take a second look at 2 Kings 9:30.

When Jehu came to Jezreel, Jezebel heard about it, so she painted her eyes, fixed her hair, and looked down from the window.

Makeup and cute hair are not sinful, but when we use them to draw attention to ourselves rather than shining the spotlight on God, we miss the mark as image bearers. Jezebel's story points to the gospel by showing us how ugly our sin nature truly is.

When we worship something or someone other than Jesus—we are like Jezebel. When we hate our fellow image bearers—we are like Jezebel. When we use our beauty to manipulate others—we are like Jezebel. When our pride trips us up—we are like Jezebel.

Take a moment to confess to God any ways you see yourself in Jezebel's story. Ask for His help to live more like Him and less like Jezebel in each area.

God Pursues: A Beautiful Romance

*Israel, return to the Lord your God,
for you have stumbled in your iniquity.*
HOSEA 14:1

STRETCH

Here's a request I love to make of Christians who are older than me: "Tell me about that time God let you down."

I've been asking that question for years, almost every chance I get to hang out with people with a gray hair or two. I've never met a single person with an answer. Instead, they all gush about God's faithfulness, telling me how time and time again He has shown up in their lives.

When we learn to pay attention to the stories of others around us and to always be on the lookout for how all stories point to God, we become aware of this truth:

> *For the Lord is good, and his faithful love endures forever; his faithfulness, through all generations.* **PSALM 100:5**

It's sometimes difficult to see God's hand in the day to day challenges of our lives, but when we glance in the rearview mirror, it becomes obvious He has loved us faithfully all along. When we practice inverting the pyramid by looking for the character of God and the realities of the gospel in every person's story, we see redemption written on every page of history.

Armed with that knowledge, I think you're ready for your first real assignment. I want you to interview an older Christian who has followed Christ for at least twenty years. Ask them to tell you about the time God let them down. I'm confident they won't have an answer, but they will be able to point you to God's faithfulness.

Write about what you learned and then share your experience with your group.

STORY I.D.

Fill in the Story I.D. chart for Gomer. You can read about her in Hosea 1.

Who	Gomer
What	
When	
Where	
Why	

DIGGING DEEPER

Before we dig too deep into Gomer's story, we need a few reminders. Fill in the blanks for the truths we've already uncovered in this study.

All people bear the image of _____ (Gen. 1:27).

_____ Scripture is God-breathed and useful for instruction (2 Tim. 3:16).

God takes our _____ and makes it our _____ (Ps. 51:13-14).

These truths are critical to helping us understand Gomer's story. It is not an easy story to read or understand. There are parts of her story that will make us squirm and other parts that may be difficult to understand, but when we look at it through the lens of the gospel, we see it is one of the greatest stories ever told. Let's jump in.

Hosea was a prophet. Based on what you've already learned in this study, what does God use prophets to do? (Think of Deborah, Nathan, and Elijah.)

As we've worked our way through the Old Testament, we've seen this pattern emerge:

- God makes a bold promise to His people.
- The people rebel and worship other gods.
- God appoints a prophet to confront wickedness and call His people back to pure worship.
- The people repent.
- The cycle repeats.

List any examples of this cycle we've investigated so far in this study.

Hosea 1:1 tells us that Hosea prophesied during the reigns of Uzziah, Jotham, Ahaz, Hezekiah, and Jeroboam. Look up the following verses and determine whether each ruler was a good king who followed the one true

God, or a bad king who worshiped idols. Place an X in the correct column for each king.

	Good King	Bad King
Uzziah (2 Chron. 26:3-4)		
Jotham (2 Kings 15:33-34)		
Ahaz (2 Kings 16:2-3)		
Hezekiah (2 Kings 18:2-3)		
Jeroboam (1 Kings 13:33)		

Hosea had seen his people led by good kings and bad kings. He'd been with God's people through times of rebellion and times of faithfulness. Yet, God's plan is not for our faith to rise and dip like a mountain range. We aren't to love and follow Him one moment and turn our backs on Him the next. It's not God's plan for our worship to be pure when the culture affirms it, but turn toward idols when someone takes power who doesn't acknowledge the one true God. God is faithful in every circumstance and throughout every generation. Gomer's story pulls a giant magnifying glass over our often wayward and destructive response.

Illustrate your faith in the form of a line. Is it a straight incline upward, trusting God more and more each day? Does it look more like a line graph with sharp peaks and deep valleys? Does it look like the circle we see in the faith of the Israelites: trust, sin, repent, repeat?

A BEAUTIFUL, BROKEN PICTURE

God gave Hosea specific instructions about his family. Let's pick out the specifics.

According to Hosea 1:2, what kind of wife was Hosea asked to pursue?

What was this marriage designed to represent?

Next, God instructed Hosea to give his children three very strange names (Hos. 1). I doubt Jezreel is a name we will find in any baby book. This name takes us back to Jezebel's story. Jehu was the ruler who ordered Jezebel to be thrown from her window. He also killed all of King Ahab's sons (2 Kings 10:1-17) and had their heads shipped to him in the city of Jezreel (2 Kings 10:7). Jehu did not follow God with all of his heart (2 Kings 10:31). Hosea named his first baby boy after a murderous king who did not follow God faithfully.

This is already a picture of a pain-filled and fractured family, but it gets worse. Hosea 2 used Hosea and Gomer's marriage to highlight Israel's unfaithfulness. Gomer abandoned her husband and chased other lovers she hoped would satisfy her. Just like the Israelites worshiped golden calves or like we may worship performance, perfection, or attention, Gomer abandoned the one who could meet her deepest needs for those who never could.

In Hosea 3, God commanded Hosea to take dramatic action in response. Read the entire chapter.

What did Hosea do for Gomer?

He bought her back! Review the definition for redeem.

This is exactly what God commanded Hosea to do for his wife. Look at the text again. What price did Hosea pay to repurchase his wife (v. 2)?

Even though Gomer was unfaithful and chased after other lovers, Hosea paid a huge price to buy her back, to redeem her. The details are so dramatic, that it's easy to get hung up on the lower story, but look up. This is not a story about an unfaithful wife and the husband who pursued her. It's a picture of a much higher truth.

Fill in the blanks for 1 Corinthians 6:20.

For _____ were _____ at a _____. So glorify _____ with your body. **1 CORINTHIANS 6:20**

Just like Gomer was purchased by her husband, you have been bought with a price. The cost to redeem us was so much more than a few pieces of silver and a bag of barley.

According to Ephesians 1:7, how do we receive redemption?

Jesus' death on the cross was the price paid to repurchase us, to buy us back from slavery to sin—a price Christ willingly paid. We'll talk more about what motivated Christ to pay such a heavy price for our redemption in your devotions this week, for now lets fast-forward to the end of Gomer's story.

Chapter after chapter, Hosea focused on the rebellion of God's people that Gomer and Hosea's marriage was designed to illustrate, yet true to His loving character, God ended the story with a love letter. The final chapter of the Book of Hosea is a passionate plea to return to God, full of beautiful promises. Rather than studying this chapter like a journalist, read it like the love letter that it is.

Read Hosea 14. Circle every promise God makes in these verses.

TALK ABOUT IT

Discuss the following questions with your group:

Why do you think God used such a graphic illustration in Gomer and Hosea's marriage to communicate the story of redemption?

How does your own life tell the story of the gospel like Gomer's does?

THINK ABOUT IT

Rewrite the final verse of the Book of Hosea in your own words and journal a prayer in response.

Let whoever is wise understand these things, and whoever is insightful recognize them. For the ways of the LORD are right, and the righteous walk in them, but the rebellious stumble in them. **HOSEA 14:9**

Who? Runaway Bride

I got married on the beach at sunset. It was hands down the most romantic day of my life. *Swoon*! But the night before was a little less rosy. I knew I had picked the right guy, but I didn't know if I was really marriage material. *Will I be a good wife?* I wondered.

More than fifteen years later, I'm so glad I chose to walk down the aisle (or in my case, the sandy beach) toward my groom. What a tragedy it would have been if I had let my cold feet march me in the other direction, yet this is exactly what we see God's people do over and over again.

As you read the stories of these women and see how often Israel rebelled against God's commands or questioned the promises of God, do you ever wonder why He chose them? I do! And yet, how does God describe the Israelites in Deuteronomy 7:6? They were chosen. They were treasured. They were set apart.

When we peel back the layers of each woman's story, we often see the themes of rebellion and rejection. Many of them could be renamed after Gomer's daughter, "No Mercy" or her son, "Not My People." These are the labels God's people often deserve. So, why did He choose Israel? Why did He call them His treasured possession? Let's keep reading in Deuteronomy 7 for the answer.

Write out Deuteronomy 7:8.

God didn't choose Israel as His own because they were mighty, but because they were weak. God was never surprised by their doubt and sin. He is sovereign after all. He sees all of history from beginning to end. Israel's rebellion is the just the lower story. God picked a small, weak, wayward group as His own to tell the higher story, the gospel story.

In the same way, God calls us His bride (more on that tomorrow), not because we deserve it or because we're great marriage material. He is motivated by His love for us, not our ability to follow the rules and always trust His promises.

HOW WEAK POINTS TO STRONG

It's tempting to distort the gospel, to convince ourselves that if we just follow the right rules, wear (or don't wear) the right clothes, and make the right choices, we can earn God's love and acceptance. But the beautiful truth of the gospel is that we are not strong enough to follow God faithfully. We are all prone to live like runaway brides, fleeing the love story God has written for us.

Gomer's story helps us see the truth more clearly. God doesn't love us because we are faithful, but because He is. He doesn't keep us because we follow Him perfectly, yet He redeems us because we are His.

Write out Romans 5:6 in your own words.

Just like Hosea proposed to Gomer when she was still a prostitute, Christ died for us before we changed our ways. We did not earn His grace. We do not deserve it, but He lavishes it upon us because He loves us like a groom loves his bride. Israel's weakness shines a spotlight on God's strength. That's why He chose them. That's the lower story. Our weakness shines a spotlight on God's strength. He is the higher story.

In 2 Corinthians 12:9, how did the apostle Paul respond to his weakness?

He bragged about it! Since Paul understood that every area of weakness in his life provided an opportunity to display God's strength, he embraced his weaknesses.

What areas of weakness do you see in your own life?

How could each of these areas showcase God's strength?

DAY 2) *What? The Perfect Ending*

Gomer's story is just one example where marriage is used as an object lesson to describe God's love for us. You may be years away from walking down the aisle as a bride yourself, but let's think about marriage for a moment. Instead of considering flowers and gowns, let's consider how marriage points to the higher story.

Ephesians 5:22-31 gives practical instructions for married couples. Go ahead and give that passage a quick skim. In verse 32, we see that while Paul's words have practical implications, he was not primarily writing instructions for married couples. Marriage is a picture designed to tell a story. The point of the story is not the bride and groom, but about Christ and His church. The goal of marriage isn't simply to live happily ever after, but to bear the image of God by showcasing the profound mystery of the gospel.

BACK TO THE GARDEN

Let's go all the way back to the Garden and check on Eve. Review Genesis 2:18-25. Here are the highlights:

- Adam was alone and it was "not good" (v. 18).
- Adam had companions of every shape and size, but he needed someone who would be a helper fit for him (v. 20).
- God formed a woman from the man (v. 21).
- God brought the woman to the man (v. 22).

And Adam gushes some of the most romantic words ever written in verse 23. "At last!" Adam exclaimed. It was as if he said, "I have been waiting for you all my life." Which wasn't very long, but it must have felt like it. Adam knew what it was like to wait for love. We just witnessed the first wedding ever. God was telling Adam and Eve that they were one. Their instructions were to cling to each other in good times and in bad.

Fast forward to the end of your Bible, to the Book of Revelation. Read Revelation 19:6-9.

What marriage is described in this verse?

Genesis tells the story of a simple wedding. The only ones in attendance were Adam, (the groom), Eve (the bride), and God (the wedding officiate). Revelation tells of a grand affair. There are so many in attendance that their voices sound like mighty peals of thunder. The bride is spectacular, clothed in blinding white garments. This is the biggest event in history. This is not a wedding to be missed!

Sure, the wedding in Revelation sounds romantic, but we miss something big if we don't catch who is getting married here. This is a wedding between "the Lamb" and "his Bride" (v. 7). Jesus is the groom, and those of us who follow Him are His bride. He died so that we could be clothed in beautiful, white wedding clothes instead of the filthy rags our sin wraps us up in.

A PERFECT ENDING

Every good story needs a perfect ending. God has already written one for us. I don't know how the story of your life will go. I don't know if you'll get to a plan a wedding or pick rice out of your hair. But I know that if you follow Jesus, your wedding day is coming. There will be so many people there that their voices will sound like thunder. The groom will be beaming. He has waited for this moment for an eternity.

Before I set you off to consider the wedding feast on your own, there's a little detail I'm dying to show you. Read Revelation 19:7-8 again. This is a beautiful description of the bride in her wedding dress.

> What words are used to describe the gown she clothed herself with?

Look again. How did she get the dress? It was *given* to her. She didn't save her money and go out and buy it. She didn't earn it. It was a gift, given to her by her groom. Again, who is the Bride this passage describes? Us, the church! Who is the groom? Jesus! Through His sacrifice on the cross, He purchased our wedding dress. What a beautiful picture of redemption!

> Spend some time meditating on Revelation 19:6-10. Ask the Lord to help you see the marriages around you and your own future marriage as a portrait of the beautiful promise of what is to come.

Why?
God's Unrelenting Love

Describe a time when you were betrayed by a boyfriend, friend, or family member. What happened to that relationship?

Hosea faced the ultimate betrayal. Though he loved his wife sacrificially, she ran away from him and pursued other men. From a human standpoint, Hosea seems justified in divorcing his wife and marrying another woman. Instead, he redeemed her and stayed faithful to her.

With Hosea and Gomer's story as the backdrop, Hosea 2:14-23 describes God's deep and persistent love toward His people. God announces several betrothals (or promises) in verses 19-20. Fill in the blanks for each one.

I will take you to be my _____ forever.

I will take you to be my wife in _____,
_____, _____, and _____.

I will take you to be my wife in _____,
and you will know the LORD.

This is the motivation behind all of God's promises. This is the reason He keeps them. This is the reason God redeemed us from sin. This is the reason He is preparing a wedding feast for us.

He is motivated by steadfast love. Use a thesaurus to list a few synonyms for the word *steadfast*.

Now, list several examples of antonyms of the word *steadfast*.

God's love for us is not fickle or flighty. It is steadfast, unmovable, unchanging. He loves us because He created us in His image. He redeems us because He longs to be with us for eternity.

God's love toward us is like no other love we've ever experienced. It's the kind of love that chases us down when we run away, forgives us when we've sinned, and welcomes us home when we don't deserve it.

In Gomer's story, God's love was illustrated in a marriage. In the Book of Luke, Jesus used a parable about a father and his sons to teach the same truth.

Read Luke 15:11-32.

How do you see God's steadfast love on display in this story? Look past the lower story. How does each of the following characters point to the higher story:

The father:

The prodigal son:

The son who stayed home:

THIS CHANGES EVERYTHING

Because we are sinners living in a broken world, God's steadfast love can be a difficult concept to grasp. Gomer's story and the story of the prodigal son both shine a white hot spotlight on the higher story: God's love is steadfast and unrelenting, even when we don't deserve it.

This is why we need the stories found in God's Word. They help us see truths we can't focus on in our own lives, forcing us to see God through a filter other than our feelings or circumstances.

When I feel unloved, I have a little motto I've trained my heart to say. You can say it with me: *I will measure Your love by the cross and Your power by the resurrection.*

I can know that Jesus loves me because He died for me. I can have confidence in His promises because He's never broken a single one, including His promise to raise from the dead.

He loves us. He always, always will. Living in light of that truth is a game changer.

Take some time to journal a love letter to God. Instead of focusing on His steadfast love for you, list all the reasons you love Him back.

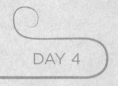

DAY 4 *The Bigger Story*

Did you know that emotional heartbreak can actually harm your physical heart? It's true! *Broken Heart Syndrome* is a condition recognized by doctors as a temporary heart condition often caused by pain and loss such as a devastating break up or the death of a loved one. Patients experience a temporary disruption of normal heart function that feels like a heart attack. It is physically possible (though highly unlikely) to die of a broken heart.[1]

Though most of us won't land in the hospital with Broken Heart Syndrome, we will all experience heartache from time to time.

Write about a time when you experienced a broken heart.

A BROKEN HEARTED GOD

Gomer's story helps us see that God experiences broken hearts too.

Preacher and Bible scholar, G. Campbell Morgan, connected the dots this way:

> *No one can read the story of Hosea without realizing the agony of his heart. Then, lift the human to the level of the Infinite, and know this, that sin wounds the heart of God. I believe that the meaning of David when his great penitential Psalm he said, 'Against Thee, Thee only have I sinned.' Some one says—Was that true? Had he not sinned against Bathsheba? No, he sinned with Bathsheba. His sin against Uriah, too, was in the last analysis sin against God. His sin was of that nature that cause pain to the heart of God, and wounded love.*[2]

Maybe you've never considered the possibility of God having a broken heart, but Scripture tells us that He can. Because He loves us so much, our sin breaks His heart. And yet, He still promises to forgive us when we confess our sins (1 John 1:9).

We all have Gomer tendencies. We are prone to wander away from the One who loves us most and to seek satisfaction elsewhere. Because God loves us, He cannot tolerate our sin, yet because His love is steadfast He freely offers us forgiveness and a way back to Him. This is the strand that ties each of us together. From Eve to Gomer to me to you—our lives are each a page in the best and biggest story every told. We bear the image of a loving, faithful, promise-keeping God.

Your story is not really about you, but about the God who made you. You were designed to showcase:

- the God who speaks
- the God who sees
- the God who rescues
- the God who inspires
- the God who equips
- the God who redeems
- the God who opposes
- the God who pursues

Because of His steadfast love, our stories end like all good stories should ... *Happily ever after.*

> *Therefore, since we also have such a large cloud of witnesses surrounding us, let us lay aside every hindrance and the sin that so easily ensnares us. Let us run with endurance the race that lies before us, keeping our eyes on Jesus, the source and perfecter of our faith. For the joy that lay before him, he endured the cross, despising the shame, and sat down at the right hand of the throne of God.* HEBREWS 12:1-2

Leader Guide

Dear Girls Ministry Leader,

From the very bottom of my heart, thank *you* for investing in young women's lives using this study. Pointing girls toward God's Word and walking with them as they wrestle with big concepts like the gospel, sin, and redemption is no small undertaking. I'm rooting for you every step of the way.

It's true that this resource is organized around eight women whose stories are described in the Old Testament, but this is not really a study about women, it's a study about Jesus. The big idea you'll see woven throughout each session is that our stories are the lower story. As image-bearers of God, we are all are designed to showcase the higher story, the gospel story.

I think it's fair to warn you that this study highlights some tricky sections of Scripture. We'll walk through Bathsheba's adulterous affair, Jezebel's gory death, and Gomer's choice to prostitute herself rather than remain faithful to her husband—sections of this study may cause you and your girls to squirm. Since 2 Timothy 3:16 assures us all Scripture is God-breathed and useful for our instruction, we don't have to skip the tricky parts of the Bible. Each story provides an opportunity to look past the messy lives of individual women and toward the Messiah. I've provided lots of tools to guide your discussion along the way. Here is a flyover of those tools and how to use them.

STRETCH

Each session begins with a short stretch section. Like the warm up before a work out, this section is designed to get the reader's blood flowing and help her develop the muscles needed to become a lifelong student of God's Word.

STORY I.D. CHART

Throughout the study, I encourage the reader to think like an investigator. To help with that, I've included charts in each session to help the reader examine the who, what, when, where, and why of each person. Completed Story I.D. charts are included in this Leader Guide.

DIGGING DEEPER

This is the main group Bible study component for each session. Use this as your primary lesson plan for instruction each week.

TALK ABOUT IT

Group discussion questions are included at the end of each Digging Deeper section.

DAILY DEVOTIONS

Each session includes four days of daily devotions designed to help girls explore the weekly theme on their own. An optional fifth devotion is included in your Leader Guide for you to point out to your group.

My own personal motto for teaching God's Word is this: Whoever is doing the work is doing the learning. When we allow our students to wrestle with God's Word for themselves, they gain the maximum amount of wisdom and insight. There are sections of this study that may be a struggle. That's good! God's Word is strong enough for us to push up against it. Cheer your girls on as they go, but keep pointing them toward God's Word every step of the way.

I'm grateful you've invited me into the story of your group. I can't wait to open up God's Word with you and your girls.

A fan,

Erin

God Speaks: A Beautiful Beginning

CHARACTER FOCUS: Eve

ADDITIONAL CHARACTERS: Adam, Satan

KEY PASSAGES: Genesis 1–4

GETTING STARTED (OPTIONAL)

This study focuses on the stories of ten ordinary women. To help girls start thinking about the impact of stories, ask each of them to share about a story she loved when she was a little girl. This can be a story from a book, a movie, or a story told to her by her parents or grandparents.

Ask:

- Why do we love stories so much?

- Why do we remember stories so clearly?

- What are the elements of a great story?

THE BIG IDEA

As you look at this session, here are some big ideas you don't want to miss.

- Readers will practice examining Biblical texts using the journalism principle of the inverted pyramid. This helps us look for the most important details first.

- When we study God's Word, the most important question to ask is always: What does this reveal about God?

- We were created by God (Gen. 1:1).

- We were made in the image of God (Gen. 1:27).

- God is the foremost expert on our identity.

STORY I.D. CHART

Readers will be asked to fill in Eve's Story I.D. after looking at the text. Here is an example of a completed chart.

KEY PASSAGES: Genesis 1–3

Who   Eve

What   first woman, wife to Adam, mother, sinned by disobeying God

When   at creation

Where   garden of Eden

Why   God made Eve in His image. He created her as a helper to Adam.

HOMEWORK REVIEW

Since this is your first session, there is no homework review this week.

PRAYER PROMPTS

> *Rejoice always, pray constantly, give thanks in everything; for this is God's will for you in Christ Jesus.*
> **1 THESSALONIANS 5:16-18**

Here are some ideas for how to pray *for* your girls this week.

- Pray that God would give them a desire to know His Word.
- Pray for them to see God as the main character of every story and the Author of their stories.
- Pray for them to look to God as the expert on their identity and to seek to live out His design for them.

Here are some ideas for how to pray *with* your girls this week.

- *Jesus, help us to carve out the time to seek you daily throughout this study.*
- *Jesus, help us to understand how our stories point to you.*

BONUS DEVOTION

Here is an optional fifth devotion for you to send to your girls this week.

KNOWING YOUR ENEMY

Eve's story is our first introduction to Satan (the serpent or the enemy). Review Eve's interaction with Satan in Genesis 3:1-7. Based on this passage, what words would you use to describe Satan?

Ezekiel 28:13-19 is a passage believed to describe Satan's fall. John 8:44 is another passage that describes him. Use both passages to identify the enemy. Use these questions as your guide.

Who was he?

What did/does he do?

When does his story take place?

Where is he?

First Peter 5:8 helps us understand the *why* of Satan's choices. According to this verse, what motivates him?

How do you see this play out in Eve's story?

How do you see this play out in your own story?

It is tempting to get hung up on Satan's desire to attack us, yet Eve's story reminds us that Satan is not the main character of any story. Though he does do damage to Eve by tempting her to sin, He cannot undo God's love for us or His ability to redeem us.

SESSION 2
God Sees: A Beautiful Knowing

CHARACTER FOCUS: Hagar

ADDITIONAL CHARACTERS: Sarai, Abram, Leah, Widow of Nain

KEY PASSAGE: Genesis 16

GETTING STARTED (OPTIONAL)

It's time for an old-fashioned game of "Pin the Tail on the Donkey." Premade versions can often be purchased inexpensively at party stores or you can make your own using poster board and tape. Make sure girls are blindfolded and cannot see the donkey. To up the ante, spin them around a few times before their turn. Offer a small prize to the girl who places the tail closest to the correct spot.

Say: Imagine what might happen if you had to complete the following tasks without the use of your sight.

- Putting on your makeup
- Cleaning your room
- Driving
- Doing homework

Sight matters! This week we will look at the story of Hagar, a woman who couldn't see a way out of her desperate circumstances until she encountered the God who saw her.

THE BIG IDEA

As you look at this session, here are some big ideas you don't want to miss.

- Through Hagar's story we learn that one of God's names is *El Roi* meaning "the one who sees" (Gen. 16:13).
- He knows more about us than anyone else ever could. Yes, Jesus loves me, this I know, but Jesus knows me, this I *love*!
- Psalm 139 is a "knowing Psalm," describing how well God knows us. His attention to our lives is a comfort.
- Hagar and Sarai's story illustrates the New Covenant and points to Jesus (Gal. 4:21-30).

STORY I.D. CHART

Readers will be asked to fill in Hagar's Story I.D. after looking at the text. Here is an example of a completed chart.

KEY PASSAGE: Genesis 16

Who   Hagar

What   slave, arranged marriage to Abram, hated by Sarai

When   after God's covenant with Abram

Where   desert

Why   Hagar's life was troubled because Abram and Sarai doubted God's promise and took matters into their own hands.

HOMEWORK REVIEW: SESSION 1 DEVOTIONS

DAY 1: Readers were asked to create a Story I.D. chart of themselves and to consider the influence of the enemy, Satan. Ask them to share their results.

DAY 2: How do Adam and Eve's stories showcase the theme of redemption?

DAY 3: Why does God describe Himself as the *Alpha* and *Omega*?

DAY 4: What is the gospel?

PRAYER PROMPTS

Rejoice always, pray constantly, give thanks in everything; for this is God's will for you in Christ Jesus.
1 THESSALONIANS 5:16-18

Here are some ideas for how to pray *for* your girls this week.

- Pray for them to recognize that God sees every detail of their lives and knows them better than they know themselves.
- Pray for them to understand the meaning of redemption and to recognize God's redemptive work in themselves and others.
- Pray for them to understand the gospel and respond to it.

Here are some ideas for how to pray *with* your girls this week.

- *Jesus, help us to understand that we are known and loved by You.*
- *Jesus, thank You for redeeming us from our sin.*
- *Jesus, You are the Alpha and Omega. There is none like You!*

BONUS DEVOTION

Here is an optional fifth devotion for you to send to your girls this week.

TRACING THE THREAD

Hagar was forced to marry Abram (who later became Abraham). God made an important covenant with Abraham that pointed to Jesus. Read the covenant in Genesis 15.

What specific promises did God make to Abraham?

Think of this moment like the threading of a needle. We will follow the thread through the lives of many women in this study. Over and over we will see themes like:

- God's deep love for His people.
- His redemption.
- His goodness.
- His consistency in keeping His promises.

Psalm 105 is a song of praise, describing God's faithfulness in keeping His covenant. Read through this Psalm during the week and thank God for the many promises He has kept in your life.

God Rescues: A Beautiful Song

CHARACTER FOCUS: Miriam

ADDITIONAL CHARACTERS: Moses, Shiphrah, Puah

KEY PASSAGE: Exodus 15:1-21

GETTING STARTED (OPTIONAL)

This session focuses on Moses' family and encourages readers to pay attention to the genealogies in Scripture as a map to the faithfulness of God. Ask your girls to create their own family tree. Provide art supplies such as paint, markers, poster board, and so on. Encourage them to trace their family back as far as possible. In addition to writing/illustrating the names of family members, ask them to include details about each person's faith.

Say: We'll look at God's blessings on a specific family in this session and His bigger blessings on the family of God. Miriam's family was not perfect, just like your family is not perfect, yet God uses all families to teach us who He is.

THE BIG IDEA

As you look at this session, here are some big ideas you don't want to miss.

- All Scripture is God-breathed and useful (2 Tim. 3:16).
- God is our Deliverer, and Jesus is our Savior.
- In response to God's deliverance, we should worship.
- We are called to fear God, not man.
- Both Moses and Jesus were born under an edict of death. The plans of God cannot be stopped.

STORY I.D. CHART

Readers will be asked to fill in Miriam's Story I.D. after looking at the text. Here is an example of a completed chart.

KEY PASSAGES: Exodus 15:1-21; Numbers 20:1; 26:59; 1 Chronicles 6:3

Who	Miriam
What	daughter of Jochbed, sister of Moses and Aaron, fled with Moses and millions of God's people
When	during the reign of Pharaoh in Egypt, the exodus
Where	Egypt, the wilderness
Why	worshiped God because of His great rescue

HOMEWORK REVIEW: SESSION 2 DEVOTIONS

DAY 1: Readers were asked to chart Leah and the Widow of Nain. Here are completed charts for each woman.

Leah's story is found in Genesis 29–33. The widow of Nain's story is found in Luke 7:11-17.

Who	Leah	Widow of Nain
What	daughter of Laban, sister of Rachel, wife of Jacob, less beautiful than her sister, mother	widow, her only son had died
When	after Abraham and Isaac, before Joseph	during Jesus' earthly ministry
Where	Paddan Aram	Nain
Why	God saw Leah's pain and blessed her.	God saw the widow's suffering and had compassion on her.

DAY 2: This devotion ended with a prayer declaring that God can handle our worries. What worry did you write about?

DAY 3: What is your reaction to the truth that God sees your past and your future?

DAY 4: This devotion asked you to make a declaration: *I am not a slave to sin. I am a child of the promise.* What does this mean? Let's say it together.

YER PROMPTS

Rejoice always, pray constantly, give thanks in everything; for this is God's will for you in Christ Jesus.
1 THESSALONIANS 5:16-18

Here are some ideas for how to pray *for* your girls this week.

- Pray that they would see all Scripture as inspired and important rather than choosing only some sections to believe and apply.
- Pray that they would see Jesus as their Deliverer and their Savior.
- Pray that they would worship Him like Miriam did.

Here are some ideas for how to pray *with* your girls this week.

- *Jesus, help us to understand Your Word and to run toward it as the source of truth.*
- *Jesus, we worship You for all You have done for us. Thank You!*
- *Jesus, teach us to be humble so that You can use us to lead Your people.*

BONUS DEVOTION

Here is an optional fifth devotion for you to send to your girls this week.

SING!

Use an Internet search to fill out a bonus Story I.D. chart on Fanny Crosby.

Who   Fanny Crosby

What

When

Where

Why

Fanny wrote more than 9,000 hymns and songs! Can you imagine? Maybe you've even sung some of Fanny's lyrics in church. She actually wrote one of my favorite hymns, "To God be the Glory."[1] Look up the song and listen to it if you haven't heard it before.

How would you describe Fanny's attitude toward God based on these words?

Fanny reminds me of Miriam. Though physically blind, she could see all God had done for her. Her response was to worship through song. She wrote so many songs, it seems she couldn't stop singing about God and His faithfulness.

Set aside 15 minutes to worship God through music this week. You can blast your favorite praise music, take a walk and sing your favorite hymns, or take an approach more like Fanny's and write a worship song of your own.

SESSION 4
God Inspires: A Beautiful Trust

CHARACTER FOCUS: Deborah

ADDITIONAL CHARACTERS: Barak

KEY PASSAGES: Judges 4–5

GETTING STARTER (OPTIONAL)

This session encourages readers to cheer for one another. To help them practice, tape a piece of paper on each girl's back. Instruct the group to write words of affirmation on each others' paper focusing on God's given gifts and talents (rather than external beauty).

Say: This week we'll look at the story of Deborah. Deborah championed others by recognizing their gifts and encouraging them to live like God called them to live. Let's do the same for each other!

THE BIG IDEA

As you look at this session, here are some big ideas you don't want to miss.

- We can do what God calls us to do because He is with us.
- We can champion each other and encourage each other to live like God calls us to.
- Feelings aren't facts. We can trust God more than our emotions.
- Our willingness to submit to human authority is the greatest indicator of our willingness to submit to God's authority.
- The cross is the down payment for the promises of God.

STORY I.D. CHART

Readers will be asked to fill in Deborah's Story I.D. after looking at the text. Here is an example of a completed chart.

KEY PASSAGE: Judges 4–5

Who	Deborah
What	wife, prophetess, poet, judge, warrior
When	during the reign of Jabin
Where	Canaan
Why	Because Deborah was devoted to God, she encouraged others to live like He called them to.

HOMEWORK REVIEW: SESSION 3 DEVOTIONS

DAY 1: Readers were asked to chart Shiphrah and Puah. Here is an example of a completed chart.

Who	Shiphrah and Puah
What	Hebrew midwives
When	during the reign of Pharaoh
Where	Egypt
Why	Because they feared God more than man, they disobeyed Pharaoh's orders to kill Hebrew babies.

DAY 2: What made Moses a great leader?

DAY 3: What did you learn about the plans of God?

DAY 4: Review Romans 6:6-8. What did Jesus save us from?

PRAYER PROMPTS

Rejoice always, pray constantly, give thanks in everything; for this is God's will for you in Christ Jesus.
1 THESSALONIANS 5:16-18

Here are some ideas for how to pray *for* your girls this week.

- Pray that they would be wise, discerning, and bold like Deborah.
- Pray that they would learn to champion each other rather than compare.

- Pray that they would understand that all authority is God-given and willingly submit to both their human authorities and God's authority.

Here are some ideas for how to pray *with* your girls this week.

- *Jesus, help us to live like You have called us to live even when we are afraid.*
- *Jesus, show us how to use our words to be life-givers.*
- *Thank You for the cross. Help us to remember that it is the down payment for all of your promises.*

BONUS DEVOTION

Here is an optional fifth devotion for you to send to your girls this week.

EMBRACING YOUR MISSION

Deborah trusted God, embraced her mission, and was victorious. She inspires us to trust Christ and embrace our own mission.

Read Matthew 28:16-20. What specific assignments does Jesus give to His followers in this passage?

This is the mission God has for each of us. (It's often referred to as the Great Commission). It doesn't matter how old we are, where we live, or whether or not we feel ready to share God's Word—God asks us to tell others about Him.

Like Deborah, we need to trust Christ, embrace the mission, and trust His promised victory. One way to fulfill the Great Commission is simply to tell the story of what God has done for you.

What does 1 Peter 3:15 ask us to do?

You don't have to have the Bible memorized to share the gospel, you simply need to be prepared to share what God has done in your life. Practice this week by writing out your testimony. Then, ask God to give you opportunities to fulfill your mission by sharing your story with others.

God Equips: A Beautiful Calling

CHARACTER FOCUS: Abigail

ADDITIONAL CHARACTERS: Nabal, David

KEY PASSAGE: 1 Samuel 25

GETTING STARTED (OPTIONAL)

This session looks at Jesus' call to be peacemakers by examining the life of Abigail. To get your group thinking about conflict and peace, engage in a game of speed tic-tac-toe. Place girls in two rows facing each other with paper and pens in between each pair. Announce that they will have thirty seconds to try to win a game of tic-tac-toe. Once thirty seconds have passed announce that they are to switch partners and try again. Rotate through several pairs.

Say: Competition and conflict feel harmless in a quick game of tic-tac-toe, but that's not always true in our everyday lives. In this session, we'll look at the life of Abigail. She stepped in when a conflict between her husband and David became very competitive. She shows us the beauty of being humble peacemakers.

THE BIG IDEA

As you look at this session, here are some big ideas you don't want to miss.

- God calls us to be humble peacemakers.
- We need God's help to face difficult people gracefully.
- Our response to conflict exposes our trust (or lack of trust) in God.

STORY I.D. CHART

Readers will be asked to fill in Abigail's Story I.D. after looking at the text. Here is an example of a completed chart.

KEY PASSAGE: 1 Samuel 25

Who　Abigail

What　wife of Nabal, became David's wife when Nabal died

When　after Samuel died, before David took the throne

Where　Carmel

Why　Because Abigail trusted God she responded to conflict with kindness and humility. She was a peacemaker.

HOMEWORK REVIEW: SESSION 4 DEVOTIONS

DAY 1: How can you be a life-giver this week?

DAY 2: Revisit the *Feelings vs. Faith* quiz from your Day 2 Devotion. Do you tend to be more driven by feelings or faith?

DAY 3: Which authorities do you struggle to submit to? How can we hold you accountable?

DAY 4: What is your favorite promise of God from this section?

PRAYER PROMPTS

> *Rejoice always, pray constantly, give thanks in everything; for this is God's will for you in Christ Jesus.*
> **1 THESSALONIANS 5:16-18**

Here are some ideas for how to pray *for* your girls this week.

* Pray that God would teach them to value humility rather than seeking the spotlight.
* Pray for God to teach them to lean on His promises more than their feelings or circumstances.
* Pray for God to help them to respond to conflict like Abigail did, by trusting God and treating others well.

Here are some ideas for how to pray *with* your girls this week.

- *Jesus, help us to be humble and kind.*
- *Jesus, teach us to lean on You when we face conflict.*

BONUS DEVOTION

Here is an optional fifth devotion for you to send to your girls this week.

HEADING INTO HOSTILE TERRITORY

Complete a Story I.D. chart for Lottie Moon. You can do a Google search to learn about her life.

Who   Lottie Moon

What

When

Where

Why

Lottie was a young woman who left the behind the life she knew in order to be a peacemaker. Though China was hostile toward Christianity at the time, and even hostile toward Lottie, she stayed in the country and pointed the people of China toward Christ for more than thirty years.[2]

You may not be called to hop on a boat and head to a country that is hostile to Christ, but you are called to be a peacemaker.

How can you follow Lottie's example and extend grace and kindness to others in Jesus' name this week?

SESSION 6

God Redeems: A Beautiful Mess

CHARACTER FOCUS: Bathsheba

ADDITIONAL CHARACTERS: David, Uriah, Nathan

KEY PASSAGE: 2 Samuel 11

GETTING STARTED (OPTIONAL)

This session focuses on how God can redeem our messes. To get girls thinking about their spiritual and relational messes, let's get a little messy with a twist on finger painting—toe painting!

Lay large sheets of paper on the floor. Place finger paint on plates or trays on the paper and ask girls to create a masterpiece using only their toes. You can give them a specific assignment like painting the Grand Canyon or a self-portrait to make it more challenging. Have buckets of soapy water or wipes nearby for cleanup.

Say: I don't think any of you will have requests for a commissioned toe-painting any time soon. In this session, we'll look at how God can redeem the messes we make with our lives (not our toes).

THE BIG IDEA

As you look at this session, here are some big ideas you don't want to miss.

- God can turn our messes into a message about Him.
- Redemption means to restore or set right.
- God offers us plentiful redemption through Christ.

STORY I.D. CHART

Readers will be asked to fill in Bathsheba's Story I.D. after looking at the text. Here is an example of a completed chart.

KEY PASSAGE: 2 Samuel 11

Who Bathsheba

What wife of Uriah, wife to David after Uriah's death, mother of Solomon

When during the reign of King David

Where Jerusalem

Why Bathsheba was involved in an affair with David. David had her husband, Uriah, killed. Her baby son died. Yet, God brought redemption through her family.

HOMEWORK REVIEW: SESSION 5 DEVOTIONS

DAY 1: What does it mean to be a peacemaker?

DAY 2: How do we pray for someone who is stuck in sin?

DAY 3: How does God's Word ask us to respond when we hurt others with our words?

DAY 4: Review Matthew 12:36. How are you most tempted to use careless words?

PRAYER PROMPTS

Rejoice always, pray constantly, give thanks in everything; for this is God's will for you in Christ Jesus.
1 THESSALONIANS 5:16-18

Here are some ideas for how to pray *for* your girls this week.

- Pray for them to drag their messes into the light by confessing them both to Jesus and to a wise, older Christian.
- Pray for them to embrace the messy parts of their lives as an opportunity to point to the Messiah.

Here are some ideas for how to pray *with* your girls this week.

- *Jesus, help us to bring our messes to You, rather than trying to clean them up ourselves.*
- *Jesus, help us to realize that You don't ask us to come to You mess-free, but that You promise to redeem our messes.*

BONUS DEVOTION

Here is an optional fifth devotion for you to send to your girls this week.

A HEART LIKE HIS

How does 1 Samuel 13:14 describe David?

This seems like a strange description for a man who had an affair and caused another man's murder, yet despite David's messy life, God used him in big ways. Look up the following passages and list David's accomplishments from each.

1 Samuel 17

2 Samuel 5:4

2 Samuel 5:17-21

2 Samuel 6:2-4

Matthew 1:1

David began his life as a simple shepherd. He made some bad choices along the way, yet David's legacy is that he built his kingdom, defeated his enemies, and led his people toward a pure worship of God. David stood apart from the other kings of Israel, not because of the details of his own life, but because he desired to live for God's glory.

Psalm 138 was written by David to praise God. Read through the entire Psalm once or twice, and then record your own version in your journal, expressing your desire to live your life for God.

SESSION 7

God Opposes: A Beautiful Showdown

CHARACTER FOCUS: Jezebel

ADDITIONAL CHARACTERS: Ahab, Elijah

KEY PASSAGES: 1 Kings 18–21; 2 Kings 9

GETTING STARTED (OPTIONAL)

In this session, you will explore God's opposition to pride through the story of Jezebel. To illustrate this truth, complete a simple activity using marbles. Give each girl two marbles. Ask them to set one marble on a flat surface, such as a table or desk. Then instruct them to push the second marble into the first marble. What happens every time the marbles collide?

Say: In this session, we will learn what happens when our pride collides with God by looking at the story of Jezebel. Scripture tells us God opposes the proud, which means He works against us when we are prideful, much like one marble crashing into another.

THE BIG IDEA

As you look at this session, here are some big ideas you don't want to miss.

- God's Word, His church, and His people are permanent. Everything else is temporary.
- God opposes the proud.

STORY I.D. CHART

Readers will be asked to fill in Story I.D. charts for Jezebel and Ahab after looking at the text. Here is an example of a completed chart.

KEY PASSAGES: 1 Kings 16:29-34; 17–21; 2 Kings 9

Who	Jezebel	Ahab
What	daughter of Ethbaal, wife of King Ahab, promoted worship of false gods	son of Omri, husband of Jezebel, wicked king of Israel
When	during the reign of King Ahab	reigned 22 years
Where	Israel	Israel
Why	God opposed Jezebel because of her pride. She opposed Elijah because he called the nation back to pure worship of God.	Along with his wife, Jezebel, he led God's people toward the worship of the false god Baal.

HOMEWORK REVIEW: SESSION 6 DEVOTIONS

DAY 1: What messes have you seen God use from your life?

DAY 2: Who can you think of who needs to be comforted? What can you do to reach out to them this week?

DAY 3: What is something you are waiting for God on? How can we pray for you as you wait?

DAY 4: Moving forward, how do you plan to use your messes to point to the Messiah?

PRAYER PROMPTS

Rejoice always, pray constantly, give thanks in everything; for this is God's will for you in Christ Jesus.
1 THESSALONIANS 5:16-18

Here are some ideas for how to pray *for* your girls this week.

- Pray for them to reject pride and embrace humility.
- Pray for God to expose any idols in their lives and give them a desire to turn from them.

Here are some ideas for how to pray *with* your girls this week.

- *Jesus, Your Word says You resist the proud. Help us not to be proud, but humble.*

- *Jesus, help us to worship You alone.*

- *Jesus, help us to trust that nothing can stop Your plans.*

BONUS DEVOTION

Here is an optional fifth devotion for you to send to your girls this week.

PASSING THE TORCH

Ahab and Jezebel's legacy was squashed by their pride. Because of their rebellion against Him, God wiped their family off the map. Yet, Elijah's legacy lived on. Revisit the dramatic story of Elijah being taken into heaven from 2 Kings 2:1-12. Before Elijah went to heave in a chariot of fire, he appointed his successor, Elisha to continue the work he had started.

What did Elisha ask Elijah for in verse 9?

Elisha wanted the power to do more in God's name than his hero had. He got it! Here are just a few examples of the miracles God used Elisha to accomplish. Look up the following verses and describe the miracle found in each.

2 Kings 2:14

2 Kings 2:21

2 Kings 4:1-7

2 Kings 4:30-35

2 Kings 5:1-14

2 Kings 6:18

2 Kings 13:21

Go back and highlight any of Elisha's miracles that were similar to Elijah's. God used Elisha to carry on the work that He started with Elijah.

How are you passing on the torch of faith? Do you have an "Elisha" in your life who is learning about serving God through your example? If not, pray for God to give you this kind of influence.

SESSION 8

God Pursues: A Beautiful Romance

CHARACTER FOCUS: Gomer

ADDITIONAL CHARACTERS: Hosea

KEY PASSAGES: Hosea 1; 3; 14

GETTING STARTED (OPTIONAL)

In this final session, you will look at how God pursues us against all odds. Both in the group session and in their individual study, girls will look at the parallels between human marriage and God's relationship with the church, His bride. To set the tone, ask girls to brainstorm a list of their favorite romantic movies of all times.

Discuss:

- What makes a great love story?
- What do you hope your love story is like?
- Who is someone you know personally with an amazing love story?

THE BIG IDEA

As you look at this session, here are some big ideas you don't want to miss.

- Despite our rebellion, God loves us with an everlasting, steadfast love.
- Jesus has bought us back through His sacrifice on the cross.
- Our lives tell the story of the gospel.

STORY I.D. CHART

Readers will be asked to fill in a Story I.D. chart for Gomer after looking at the text. Here is an example of a completed chart.

KEY PASSAGES: Hosea 1; 3; 14

Who	Gomer
What	wife of Hosea, mother to Jezreel, Lo-ruhamah, and Lo-ammi, prostitute
When	during the reigns of Uzziah, Jotham, Ahaz, Hezekiah, and Jeroboam
Where	Israel
Why	Gomer was a prostitute who God commanded Hosea to marry as a picture of His love for us.

HOMEWORK REVIEW: SESSION 7 DEVOTIONS

DAY 1: How did Elijah respond to persecution? How do you respond when your faith is challenged?

DAY 2: How does seeing God in His throne room impact you?

DAY 3: Do you tend to obey God immediately or are you more prone to wait?

DAY 4: What similarities do you see between yourself and Jezebel?

PRAYER PROMPTS

> *Rejoice always, pray constantly, give thanks in everything; for this is God's will for you in Christ Jesus.*
> **1 THESSALONIANS 5:16-18**

Here are some ideas for how to pray *for* your girls this week.

- Pray for them to have undivided hearts for the Lord rather than rebellious ones.
- Pray for them to grasp the steadfast love of God.

Here are some ideas for how to pray *with* your girls this week.

- *Jesus, help us understand Your steadfast love for us.*
- *Jesus, help us run to You instead of others who cannot satisfy us.*

BONUS DEVOTION

Here is an optional fifth devotion for you to send to your girls this week.

ROMANTIC, REDEEMING LOVE

Much like the story of Gomer and Hosea paints a picture of God's love for us, Song of Solomon illustrates God's spectacular love toward the church, His bride. Song of Solomon is written as a poem between a bride and groom. Some of the language may feel strange to us, but the message is timeless, it is a celebration of the goodness and beauty of love.

As you finish this study, spend some time annotating Song of Solomon. Look for patterns and evidence of God's great love for you. Remember to always keep in mind the following three questions:

- What does this tell me about God?
- What does this tell me about us, the church?
- What should I do?

SESSION 9
Bonus (Optional)

Completing an 8-week study is an occasion worth celebrating! Plan a special time with your group. Here are a few ideas:

1. Meet up for pizza or ice cream.

2. Gather at the house of a leader or church member.

3. Plan a weekend away to review what God has taught you and enjoy each other's company.

SESSION 8 REVIEW

DAY 1: What does it mean to brag about our weaknesses?

DAY 2: Review the description of the marriage supper of the Lamb from Revelation 19:6-10. What are you most looking forward to about that day?

DAY 3: How does it change you to know that God loves you with an unrelenting love?

DAY 4: Did you realize that your sin breaks God's heart? How does this truth change your own attitude toward sin?

ACTIVITY IDEAS

1. Create a master timeline, tracing God's story from Eve to Gomer.

2. Ask girls to discuss their favorite character from the study. Why did they love her? Do they see themselves in her?

3. Create mosaics to illustrate how each of us is just a small part of the higher story, the gospel story.

PRAYER PROMPTS

Place the following prayer prompts on large sheets of paper around the room. Allow time for girls to move from prompt to prompt quietly, writing out their prayers beside each prompt.

Jesus, I want my story to show the world that You are...

Jesus, sometimes I forget my story is not about me. Help me to live like...

Jesus, I know You love me because...

Jesus, I see myself in the story of _____ because...

Jesus, You are the hero of my story because...

Jesus, thank You for redeeming me from...

Jesus, the gospel changes everything because...

SOURCES

SESSION 1

1. Trevin Wax, "Gospel Definitions: Tim Keller," *The Gospel Coalition*, March 7, 2008, https://blogs.thegospelcoalition.org/trevinwax/2008/03/07/gospel-definitions-tim-keller/.

2. John Piper, "The Gospel in 6 Minutes," *desiring God*, September 12, 2007, http://www.desiringgod.org/articles/the-gospel-in-6-minutes.

SESSION 2

1. Trent C. Butler, ed., *Holman Illustrated Bible Dictionary* (Nashville: Holman Bible Publishers, 2003), accessed May 12, 2017 via mywsb.com.

2. James Strong, *The New Strong's Expanded Exhaustive Concordance of the Bible* (Nashville: Thomas Nelson, 2010), 254.

SESSION 4

1. *Merriam-Webster OnLine*, s.v. "hermeneutic," accessed March 3, 2017, https://www.merriam-webster.com/dictionary/hermeneutic.

2. Kenneth O. Gangel and Stephen J. Bramer, *Holman Old Testament Commentary: Genesis*, ed. Max Anders (Nashville: B & H Publishing, 2002), accessed via mywsb.com.

SESSION 6

1. *Merriam-Webster OnLine*, s.v. "redeem," accessed March 14, 2017, https://www.merriam-webster.com/dictionary/redeem.

SESSION 7

1. Richard L. Strauss, "My Way—The Story of Ahab and Jezebel," *Bible.org*, June 28, 2004, https://bible.org/seriespage/7-my-way-story-ahab-and-jezebel.

2. Glenn Research Center, "Newton's Third Law Applied to Aerodynamics," *NASA*, accessed April 25, 2017, https://www.grc.nasa.gov/www/k-12/airplane/newton3.html.

SESSION 8

1. Mayo Clinic Staff, "Broken Heart Syndrome," *The Mayo Clinic*, accessed March 21, 2017, http://www.mayoclinic.org/diseases-conditions/broken-heart-syndrome/home/ovc-20264165.

2. G. Campbell Morgan, *Hosea: The Heart and Holiness of God* (Eugene: Wipf and Stock Publishers, 1998), 14.

LEADER GUIDE

1. "Fanny Crosby: Prolific and blind hymn writer," *Christianity Today*, accessed May 19, 2017, http://www.christianitytoday.com/history/people/poets/fanny-crosby.html.

2. "Who Was Lottie Moon?" *imb*, accessed March 23, 2017, https://www.imb.org/who-was-lottie-moon.

Notes

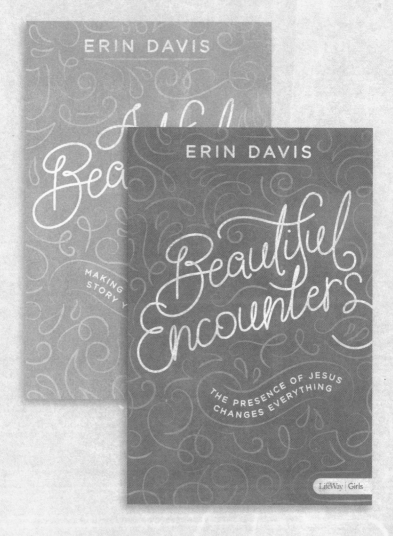